GIRL IN A BOX

GIRL IN A BOX

Seeking Enlightenment as a Tibetan Buddhist Nun

PALDROM CATHARINE COLLINS

BOOK PUBLISHING COMPANY
RHINEBECK, NEW YORK

Paperback ISBN 9781966608257
eBook ISBN 9781966608264

Library of Congress Cataloging-in-Publication Data

Names: Collins, Paldrom Catharine author
Title: Girl in a box : seeking enlightenment as a Tibetan Buddhist nun / Paldrom Catharine Collins.
Description: Rhinebeck : Monkfish Book Publishing Company, 2026.
Identifiers: LCCN 2026001323 (print) | LCCN 2026001324 (ebook) | ISBN 9781966608257 paperback | ISBN 9781966608264 ebook
Subjects: LCSH: Buddhist nuns--Religious life | Buddhist monasticism and religious orders for women | Buddhist nuns--Social conditions | Enlightenment (Buddhism)
Classification: LCC BQ6150 .C655 2026 (print) | LCC BQ6150 (ebook) | DDC 294.3/657--dc23/eng/20260120
LC record available at https://lccn.loc.gov/2026001323
LC ebook record available at https://lccn.loc.gov/2026001324

Book and cover design by Colin Rolfe

Monkfish Book Publishing Company
22 East Market Street, Suite 304
Rhinebeck, New York 12572
(845) 876-4861
monkfishpublishing.com

With unending gratitude for every teacher in this play of life.

CONTENTS

PROLOGUE

Before once upon a time, before any time at all, before past or future, before up or down, or on or off, there was no me, no you, and certainly no story to be told. Only one–all. No other existed with whom to play. So this one, in order to know itself, became two–you and me. Just that simply, the world of this and that, here and there, yes and no, good and bad, pleasure and pain was born.

And we played, this you and this me. We pretended not to know that we are really one. In order to continue our charade, our folly, we donned costumes, pretending we didn't recognize the one-self from which we sprang, the one we truly are.

We laughed and danced. We played at love, at fighting, at anger, grief, joy, gain, loss, life, death. We played for so long and so fully that eventually, we totally lost track of our oneness, the home from which we sprang.

In this daze of forgetting, in this play, in this dream, you and I began to long for something–and then to seek for what we had lost, overlooked, abandoned. Finally, amid our searching, we stopped to rest and faintly began to hear a call–come back, come home, all you who are hiding and have not yet been found.

In this moment of quiet, we knew. We remembered. It's all a dream we're playing here. We are one. You are me; and I am you.

Laughing, rolling on the ground at how we had so thoroughly tricked ourselves, we knew we were never lost, already found, already home.

INTRODUCTION

I lay stretched out flat on the cool wooden floor. I'd stopped trying to sleep sitting cross-legged in my three-foot-square meditation box, one of many ways I was failing in my endeavor to be a stellar Tibetan Buddhist nun. In this autumn of 1992, I was almost forty years old. Eight other nuns and I were locked away from the world in a retreat house in New York's Hudson Valley, encircled by a ring of stockade fencing rising twelve feet from the dusty ground. I was certain the other nuns must be sleeping, each sitting in a box in her own tiny room. Not me. I was on the floor, fighting a relentless impulse to abandon this retreat I'd promised to complete.

My teacher's voice echoed in my head, warning me that doubts—like these notions of fleeing—were demons. Up until now, I'd reasoned that such admonitions were simply scare tactics, but now my rebellious thoughts were becoming dangerous. After all, I'd spent five years striving to be right here, where I'd finally be introduced to the secret Tibetan practices leading to enlightenment.

I'd left my marriage and career for this. The leap that ended my marriage required an abandonment akin to my terrifying first jump from the high dive when I was seven. I married at eighteen, blindly certain the union would provide a container of safety, contentment, and fulfillment. Six years later my husband and I were teaching at a private school in Tulsa, Oklahoma. He taught kindergarten; I taught first grade. The perfect couple. Even though I had a kind husband, a home with a garden, and career success, discomfort rumbled. I longed for a balm to soothe an ache I couldn't fully identify. Sometimes I started sobbing and didn't know why. So, I set out on a search to find my missing happily-ever-after, an end to suffering, enlightenment.

Why enlightenment?

Perhaps it started with the fairytales. As a child, I lay on my belly on the dining room floor, clutching the royal-blue-bound volume of fables, conjuring an enchanted land–a Shangri-La. In this fantasy, my journey would end in a magical paradise with my prince, like Cinderella or Snow White. I didn't notice that life after the wedding was never mentioned.

Or maybe it was just a continuation of my parents' religious wanderings from the Southern Baptist Church, the first church our family attended. By the time I was in my teens, my father, ice clinking in his glass of scotch, was sharing his agnostic conclusions. When he heard I was on my way to a Baptist church service with my boyfriend, he rolled his eyes and scoffed, "What are you doing?" My mother had joined our neighbors in studying Theosophy, an amalgam of Buddhism and ancient Hinduism brought to the West in the late nineteenth century by a Russian aristocrat, Helena Blavatsky.

It was also the times. The possibility of transcending one's personal unhappiness wafted through the sixties and seventies like musical undulations calling a body to dance. The Beatles had traveled to India to study Transcendental Meditation with Maharishi Mahesh Yogi. Harvard professor Dr. Richard Alpert had been renamed Ram Dass by his Indian guru, Neem Karoli Baba, and was advising *Be Here Now*. And Carlos Castaneda had discovered the *Yaqui Way of Knowledge* from his teacher, Don Juan. Thus, I concluded my quest also required an enlightened master.

However, the incense-scented pages of *Autobiography of a Yogi* advised that I not go in search of my guru. What a relief. I didn't have the courage to travel to Mexico, much less to India. Somehow my holy guide was going to have to find me in Oklahoma.

A tale of widening expansion emerges as I gaze back, noting patterns in the wake of this "boat ride" of my life. At times, this stranger-than-fiction play of grace seemed ruthless. I've heard that enlightenment requires a longing as great as the need to take the next breath. Although I certainly possessed a desire to escape my perceived suffering, I wasn't naturally dauntless; rather, I was afraid to leave the nest. When I was nine, my mother had to retrieve me from my first weeklong sleep away camp after less than twenty-four hours. I fainted shortly after arriving, then woke up the next morning with a rash covering much of my body.

A few years later, I rode the roller coaster at Wedgewood Amusement Park. Its metallic wheels squealed as the shuttle car chugged to the top of a precipitous drop and then plunged over the rim. Once I stepped off the ride, the other kids got right back in line, but I didn't, vowing to never again subject myself to that unbearable sense of danger.

My life provided a just-right amount of discomfort to impel me to step outside the safety of the known into the unknown. My parents were only nineteen years old when I was born. By the time I was seven, they had three more children, two girls and a baby boy. My father gave up his dream of attending law school so he could support his growing family; his anger and absence expressed his resentment. My mother pulled into a protective shell, the natural expression of her love locked inside. I pictured her safely sealed in Tupperware. She showed her love in silence, joined the PTA, was a Girl Scout leader. But I yearned to crawl into her lap.

On this rigged human ride with perfectly imperfect parents, my feral soul was certain I could vanquish all discomfort. My strategy was first a wish to find love, to marry a fairytale prince. But when marriage didn't work, I adopted a new plan. Next, I wished for a guru, a magical wizard who could bestow enlightenment so I could transcend this messy world.

Ultimately, I've come to recognize the undeniable, yet lucky, blessing of the wounding—a fleck of sand landing (or perhaps strategically placed) in the oyster shell. The irritation producing a thing of beauty, flaming in my heart as a hymn, as a plea for redemption, as a cry for the quiet of no thought, for the embrace of God, for absolute love. I now marvel at the laser precision of the slicing which generated an underlying, yet persistent dissatisfaction. Never challenged with a real concern for food or shelter, I was given the perfect birthing ground for my search, for this tale.

From the Tibetan Buddhist perspective, discomfort is woven into the structure of this play of life. But the teachings also promise a means to end the suffering. When I first heard an explanation of the nature and cause of *dukkha* (the Sanskrit word for suffering), the descriptions seemed to fit as perfectly as Cinderella's glass slipper. Dukkha refers to the fundamental underlayer of non-satisfaction or painfulness of mundane life, like a shoe that's too tight. Buddhist texts illustrate this condition by comparing it to a cart with a slightly damaged wheel. Riding in the cart, you get a little jolt every time the wheel goes around. My strategy was to escape this dukkha by becoming like a guru on a mountaintop.

The teachings describe three types of suffering. The first is the most obvious—the suffering of clearly discernible pain, both physical and emotional. My ongoing discomfort was primarily emotional. Second is the suffering of change that arises when life's circumstances get worse (or even when they get better). And finally, the suffering of existence, or *Sankhara-Dukkha*, is defined as the subtle suffering of simply being alive, the suffering of the experience of separation. It's taught that Sankhara-Dukkha is caused by overlooking that from which all appearance arises. This belief engenders a longing to reconnect to our true nature, to have a direct experience of the mystery of life that shines through time and space.

My quest for enlightenment was initially a search for a way out, a quest to find the internal comfort I was sure others possessed. Like the sensitive princess who was left black and blue by a pea under a stack of mattresses, my suffering felt like a mass of barbed wire. This was a fairytale princess I did not wish to emulate. Since I didn't want to reveal the extent to which I was plagued by every tiny pea, I attempted to hide my emotional poverty. But at any moment it could leak out in a yearning smile.

The Tibetan texts teach that experiencing realization, or awakening, in a single moment is rare. These occurrences, when the wall of reality as we know it comes tumbling down in one fell swoop, are said to be as extraordinary as a summer snowflake. Occasionally, a big chunk of the wall might collapse. For me, the process began with splinter-like cracks in the mortar, followed by individual bricks crumbling or disappearing in an ofttimes barely a perceptible disintegration. Ultimately, the concept of a wall that collapses or a journey requiring completion has been revealed to be a perception filtered through my person-house lens. But then, without this perspective, this weaving of threads into a ribbon of time, there would be no story.

I believed the path to enlightenment required renunciation. I just needed to acquire the capacity to sit in meditative quiet for days, weeks, months, or years–long enough to somehow pop out of my mundane, unsatisfactory life. If only I could learn to meditate like the Buddha sitting under the Bodhi tree.

This tale chronicles my journey into the realm of the Tibetan Buddhist *Vajrayana* to receive teachings that in the past were only offered to Tibetan monastics in the Himalayas. Understandings didn't come in any way I'd expected. I was impelled to follow breadcrumbs scattered by my emotional reactivity, spotty rationality, naiveté, and lack of a secure sense of self. And those breadcrumbs led me to the floor of a six-by-six-foot retreat room gasping for reason, for understanding—for relief.

As the Tibetans teach, wood had been piled on the fire of my experience of the moment—the blaze illuminating the suffering of my experience of living in this body with my unavoidably troubling thoughts and emotions. The invitation is to open to the flaming. Be curious. Let go. As much as possible. Bit by bit. Again and again.

Eventually, I've come to see I was much like a girl who packs her suitcase and sets off down the road only to discover she has nowhere to go. As with Dorothy in Oz, what I was seeking, the home of my longings—had been right here all along, hiding in plain sight—masked in a cloak of the suffering I so wanted to escape. I'd overlooked it, because as the Tibetans teach: it's too simple, too obvious, too close.

Chapter One
BEING FOUND

Leaving the nest of my marriage when I was twenty-six was challenging in the daylight, but even more so at night. My bedtime companions were the books discovered in forays to the new-age bookstore. With each visit, I pushed open the stiff wooden door and the attached bell would tinkle, followed by a cloud of pungent Nag Champa incense. The wooden floorboards creaked as I squeezed through the aisles of the tiny store. I was looking for something, anything, to provide relief, to find meaning. Although I didn't fully understand the teachings in the literature I found there, like *The Lazy Man's Guide to Enlightenment* and *Be Here Now*, I was certain each held pointers for discerning my path to freedom.

One evening, as I snuggled in bed reading my latest find, *Autobiography of a Yogi*, I was particularly struck by the description of the student-teacher relationship. I closed the thick tangerine-colored paperback and studied the photo of the author on the cover. A longhaired, kind-eyed Indian guru, Paramahansa Yogananda, stared back at me. He'd wanted to search for his teacher but was instructed to first simply live his life, and his teacher would appear when he was ready. If this advice also pertained to me, then I too just needed to live my life ... and wait. But how?

I pulled the layers of blankets closer to my chin and stared at the ceiling. *Maybe there's some method or technique to speed up becoming findable. How should I live my life?*

In an initial effort to become findable, I decided to attempt meditation. Sitting on the floor of my bedroom, for fifteen minutes each day before dinner, I stared at a candle while a kitchen timer softly ticked. But after five minutes, I'd either fall asleep or want to jump out of my skin. And seductive memories of performing, of the theater, of acting, wafted into those meditation minutes.

In grade school, I discovered poetry-reciting contests. I was the eager-to-please kid hanging around my teacher. But at birthday parties, I shriveled, blending into the wall. I didn't have many friends. However, when the president of the PTA pinned a ribbon onto my dress for my poetry recitation, I was washed with a relaxation of belonging.

As a teen, I sprawled on the floor listening to the recordings of Broadway showtunes–*My Fair Lady, Oklahoma, The Sound of Music, The King and I, South Pacific*. I lolled there, floating on the waves of the music, imagining taking bows after my successful performance. By high school, I was competing in statewide speech contests and was cast in school plays and local community theater productions. Days prior to stepping in front of the audience, a fearful constriction would lodge behind my belly button, intensifying in the hours leading up to the show. But the balm of the performance trumped my stage fright. Although this fear overwhelmed me as much as riding the roller coaster, I was willing to get back in line for this ride.

In my senior year of high school when I played Anne Frank, I watched myself melt into her loves, fears, beliefs, wishes, and desires. And as I did, I noticed that my personal preferences–the clothing I liked to wear, the guy I wanted to date, the food I enjoyed–began to change. I dared not tell anyone about this experience of a porous me-ness. Everyone else seemed to possess a solid personality. Where was mine? I certainly didn't see this as a harbinger, a tiny crack in my view of my identity. But then, I didn't recognize many of the glimpses when they appeared.

When thoughts of performing, of being on stage, repeatedly floated into my meditations and daydreams, I assumed they were clues to finding a way to "live my life." So I began auditioning for roles with local community theater groups. Frequently I won the role, often as an ingenue. I absorbed new acting expertise from each director. I learned how to use my imagination to create a backstory for my character, to understand the "why" driving her words and actions, unaware of how this skill would ultimately impact my meditation practices.

To support myself, I found work as a waitress at a health food restaurant, then eventually began cleaning houses. Waitressing and acting were both great ways to meet men. I dated a handsome knight-in shining-armor lawyer and then a wandering minstrel rock-and-roll sax player, who eventually meandered on to other women. However, I was really hoping for my wizardly guru to appear.

Failing in my attempts to master meditation, I tried yoga. In a twice-weekly class at the YMCA, I became proficient at performing plow posture, headstand, and sun salutations, but during the closing fifteen-minute meditation, I often fell asleep–another confirmation that I required specific and personal instruction from an enlightened teacher.

One afternoon, after three years of living my life and waiting to be found, I spotted a young blond girl dressed in pink. She was skipping across a parking lot, her arms flung wide. Suddenly she fell. Instantly the child's mother rushed up beside her and held out a hand. The little girl looked at her mom for a moment, then grabbed her outstretched hand. With that assistance, the child stood up, gave her mother's leg a hug, then began gleefully skipping again, now in circles around her mom.

I started to cry. *Who's going to help me? Where's my teacher? What am I doing wrong? What if "being found" is just another fantasy—like that fantasy of becoming a musical theater star.*

A few evenings later I stopped by a friend's house for a glass of wine after my waitressing shift. He walked out of the kitchen with a glass of red, my favorite, placing it in front of me. "Your friend from that Alice in Wonderland adaptation you performed in last fall is starting a new theater group. She and a guy named Dan from California are writing a musical—a fantasy fairy tale. You should check it out."

If this were a work of fiction, a sprinkling of pixie dust would land in my wine glass. His grin was so sincere, I thought I'd investigate, even though I wasn't interested in some amateurish homegrown production.

The next day, squinting in the midday sun, I cupped my hands at the sides of my face and pressed them against the plate glass window of The Open Door, a hole-in the-wall theater/coffee shop, attempting to peer inside. A small, almost empty room came into focus. At one end, ruby red velvet curtains hung from ceiling to floor, framing an unimpressive stage elevated by only a foot.

After entering, as my eyes adjusted to the darkness, I spotted a lanky man with a mop of curly brown hair playing a tune on an old upright piano. He stopped and looked up and I introduced myself.

He stood, his seven-foot height towering over me, and offered his hand. "Yes, I know who you are. I'm Dan. We're hoping you'll play the princess in this musical we've written—*The Crystal Star of Amoria.*"

I soon learned that Dan was not only a playwright and piano player, but also a singer, guitar adept, sculptor, painter, a spiritual seeker—and a teacher. The script he and my friend had written was the story of a fairy princess searching for the meaning of life.

He began playing the piano again. "Would you like to hear your character's song?"

I could only nod, as he began singing. *Here comes a wish, I can feel it in the starshine. Here comes a wish, 'twill last 'til all of time. Here comes a wish, be pure of heart in telling. Make this wish, a dreamlike wish, of the loving kind, of the loving kind.*

He then played several other songs he'd written for the play. When he finished, he turned toward me and smiled. All I could manage to utter was, "Wow."

Retrieving a copy of the script from the top of the piano, he offered it to me. "What do you say? Will you be our lead?"

He didn't ask me to read even one line ... or sing a single note. I'd never performed in a musical, so didn't say yes in the moment. But that night in my backyard, I stared at the stars, knowing I'd say yes. And that everything in my life was going to change. Even in my wildest fantasies, I couldn't imagine how accepting this role, this "living my life," would eventually lead to life in a monastery.

We began rehearsing the next week.

One evening after that first week of rehearsals, I stretched out on the shag carpeting in my best friend's living room. Roberta, my spiritual-seeking pal, didn't share my interest in the theater or performing. A professional piano tuner with short dark curly hair, olive complexion, and Cheshire cat grin, she was the steady, contemplative seeker of wisdom I so wished I could be. We'd initially bonded over the writings of Carlos Castaneda and his interactions with his shamanistic shape-shifting teacher, Don Juan.

I propped myself up onto one elbow, "You know, the stuff Dan's teaching us in rehearsals sounds kind of like what Don Juan was teaching Carlos. He's talking about chakras. And moving our energy. Focusing it so the audience can actually feel what the character is feeling."

The rows of blue and orange flames in the gas heater hissed with the faintest purr. Roberta raised her eyebrows and leaned forward with an uncharacteristic show of enthusiasm, "Really? I'd like to meet him. Could I come to a rehearsal?"

The next night she watched from the back of the room. By the end of the week, Dan recruited her to be our stage manager. And within two months, Dan and I began a sexual relationship. Soon after that, I moved into his home.

For the next two years, our small troupe wrote and performed our updated versions of fairytales. In one production, our frog (played by Roberta) didn't turn into a prince when kissed by the heroine; but was happy to remain the lovable green froggy creature he'd always been.

Dan shared insights from the spiritual teachings he'd studied–well-known masters like Muktananda, Sai Baba, Neem Karoli Baba, Da Free John, Mother Meera, and Rajneesh, as well as lesser-known gurus like Vitvan. I was particularly captivated by the picture of a Tibetan teacher perched on Dan's bookcase–as was Roberta. In the grainy photo, Chögyam Trungpa Rinpoche gazed intensely through black horn-rimmed glasses. With his shiny slicked-back hair, dressed in a suit jacket and wide tie, he looked nothing like the Dalai Lama.

Although I was interested in the wisdom teachings of all the masters Dan quoted, I felt no need to try to meet any of them. Even though Dan wasn't a master from the East, I was certain he was my wished-for teacher–and so much more. He was my home.

Chapter Two

I'M ONLY VISITING

It was only supposed to be a brief stay, a month at most, visiting Roberta at the Tibetan monastery on the Hudson River. Within a week, she'd be secluded–locked away from the world for three years. After that, we'd only be able to communicate via letters delivered once each week.

Three years earlier, we both left Oklahoma behind. Dan moved to northern Minnesota and I followed. Roberta went to New York to study with the Tibetans. Now she was entering a traditional three-year retreat at this monastery just outside of Poughkeepsie–something I could only dream about. After my visit, I was going back to Minnesota, to my familiar reality–to a world where a space shuttle could explode in the morning light, a world where Reagan and Gorbachev were discussing limiting nuclear weapons. I was thirty-four years old, but not focused on current events, not even the possibility of world peace. Rather, I was intent on returning to Dan in the land of a thousand lakes.

That was before Lama Norlha asked to see me.

I'd heard tales of how Lama Norlha, a tiny mountain of a man with the power, presence, and strength of a ferocious dinosaur, was placed in a monastery in Tibet when he was only five, completed two three-year retreats by the time he was twenty-one, and escaped from a prison camp during the Chinese takeover. He led a small group of monks out of captivity under a full moon, somehow unseen by the armed guards. Lama credited his successful escape to the one million repetitions of the prayer to *Tara*, the goddess of compassion, that he recited during the months of his imprisonment.

After fleeing the camp, Lama Norlha guided his group in a treacherous trek over the Himalayas to India. Having left the world he'd known since birth, he found a home in the ashram of Neem Karoli Baba, the guru of the Western psychedelic explorer Ram Dass. Ram Dass was the author of *Be Here Now*, one of the books I purchased back in Oklahoma at the new-age bookstore. Lama Norlha lived with Neem Karoli Baba until his teacher, Kalu Rinpoche, established a new monastery in India after also fleeing from Tibet.

Standing in the open doorway of Lama's little room, I shifted slightly from foot to foot. Afternoon light filtered through the sheer curtains. The flip of his chanting pages, his *pecha,* sounded much like the flap of my bare feet padding on the cool cement floor only moments earlier. Holding his *mala*–a Tibetan rosary–his lips moved slightly, silently repeating a *mantra* as he moved his mala beads, one by one, between his thumb and forefinger while counting the repetitions. The almost imperceptible click of his moving beads sounded like fairies playing ping-pong with silk paddles.

From the doorway, I surveyed the room. Lama Norlha was seated in his three-foot square meditation box, elevated above the floor on unpainted, six-inch-tall wooden legs. The back of the box extended just above his freshly shaved head. His arm rested on one of the padded side panels. A wooden bench holding his pecha pages sat just in front of his box. The only other pieces of furniture in the room were a single bed and a deep brown chest of drawers topped with seven palm-sized copper bowls. Each was filled with water and lined up in front of a framed picture of his teacher, Kalu Rinpoche.

Kalu Rinpoche, a highly revered lineage holder and meditation master, had given Lama Norlha the task of relocating to the

United States to establish a Tibetan Buddhist center in New York City. Kalu Rinpoche sent his other *lamas* to more tame locations, like Maui, Santa Fe, and the Pacific Northwest. But within just two years, Lama Norlha, calling on the same devotion and force of will that had driven his escape from prison, not only created a successful *dharma* center in New York City, but also established this retreat facility, a Western recreation of the monasteries he left behind in Tibet.

The first traditional Tibetan three-year retreat in North America had been held here in 1982. Now, in late 1986, the second one was about to begin ... and Roberta would be in it. She wasn't Roberta anymore though. Shortly after I arrived, she'd taken vows as a Tibetan Buddhist nun. She was now Trinley Wangmo–Powerful Activity.

Standing in Lama's doorway, I wasn't sure if I should speak. *Maybe he knows I'm here and is just finishing his chanting. Anyway, why has the head of this monastery, this guru, asked to talk to me? I'm just passing through. Is it rude to just stand staring at him? Maybe I should say something.*

Raising my eyebrows, I turned up the edges of my mouth in what I hoped was a reverent smile. "Hi Lama." I looked down at the ground. *Did I just say hi? I can't even say hello properly. Maybe I should have bowed or done three prostrations like I've learned to do when entering the shrine room.*

Lama glanced up from the pecha resting on the bench in front of his box. His smile filled his broad face. "You come. Sit."

The room was filled with soft sunshine yellow–the curtains, the padded covering of his box, even Lama's shirt. In contrast, his *zen*–the shawl-like wrap draped over one of his shoulders–was a majestic burgundy echoing the color of the painted cement floor.

I plopped down in front of Lama's box, noting how his mala dangled from his hand as his elbow rested on the side of his box.

"You working hard since you come here."

Oh, so he wants to thank me for helping.

When I first arrived, since I knew I had little aptitude for meditation, I volunteered to help get the retreat center ready for Kalu Rinpoche's visit and the upcoming retreat. Under the guidance of Dechi, a gentle, pillowy nun, with a moon-like face, originally from Canada, I learned how to tape and spackle the newly installed sheetrock on the walls of the women's retreat house kitchen. Sitting at lunch and dinner each day, the white spackling dust clinging to the hairs in my nose, I breathed in an unexpected sense of well-being.

After finishing our spackling project in the retreat house, we tackled cleaning the monastery building. I helped wash and squeegee every window, polish every piece of wood, and vacuum every inch of carpeting–several times. I learned my way around an industrial-sized, turquoise Electrolux vacuum. Using that little monster, I sucked up every particle of grime from the floors and errant dust from the corners.

During our flurry of preparations for Kalu Rinpoche's visit, Lama Norlha arranged an overnight stay at his center in New York City. Everyone at the monastery was urged to go and relax. The trip was billed as a break–a reward for our hard work. When we returned the next afternoon, I was one of the first to walk in the front door.

The entry room floor was not as tidy as we left it. Immediately I spotted a few dead roaches. But in the kitchen, brown shiny bodies littered every surface. Growing up in Oklahoma, I'd seen plenty of roaches, both alive and dead, so I knew exactly what needed to happen next. They needed to be cleaned up. Pronto.

Propelled into cleaning mode, I pulled the Electrolux out from the closet under the stairs, not for a moment pausing to remember the vows the monks and nuns had taken forbidding killing of any sort, even of insects. I didn't remember the Tibetan reverence and respect for the life of every sentient being. My only thought was to clean.

Just a few days earlier, in front of the center just after sunset, I watched one of the Tibetan lamas laughing as he gazed at a mosquito filling up with blood, his blood. He looked directly at me with an openhearted, innocent smile. Holding his arm up, he laughed, repeating one of the few English words he knew.

"Generosity."

The mosquito's body engorged, turning blood red. After drinking its fill, it flew away, very much alive.

In my cleaning frenzy, I hadn't noticed Lama Norlha or several of the nuns enter the room. But while I was unceremoniously sucking the dead roaches into the dirt-laden fluffy debris already in the Electrolux, a few of the nuns began crying at the sight of those tiny–and dead–sentient beings.

Lama Norlha approached, so I turned off the jet engine whir of the vacuum. He stepped directly in front of me. "Some nuns very upset."

I put my hands behind my back and stared at the ground, attempting to demonstrate my reverence and respect. *How could I be so brash? I wasn't being at all respectful of the lives of these little creatures. I didn't show the kind of non-violent regard the lama had shown to the mosquito. I didn't see roach killing fields, only something in need of cleaning.*

"Oh Lama. I'm sorry."

He beamed a big untroubled grin, "No problem. This good. You clean. Kalu Rinpoche bless roaches when he arrive."

As he walked away, I took a relieved breath, imagining someone building a sanctified roach coffin. The roach corpses could then be delivered to Kalu Rinpoche for his blessing.

Later I learned Lama Norlha had ordered the spraying to eradicate the roaches–that's why he sent everyone to New York City. Getting rid of the roaches certainly seemed reasonable. Even important. Lama didn't want Kalu Rinpoche to be exposed to them.

But I dared not voice my questions—*What about Lama's vow to not kill? Are there exemptions to the vows?*

But now in Lama's room, pulling my spine as erect as I could, I had no thoughts of roaches or rules. I was honored to just be in the presence of the head of the monastery.

Lama smiled. "You stay. Next week Kalu Rinpoche begins giving the empowerments for retreat practices. You stay here. Take empowerments. Maybe someday you doing retreat."

But I didn't want to stay. I absolutely was not going to stay. However, just that morning I'd called Dan. Standing on the dank cement floor of the hallway, holding the tan plastic phone receiver, I heard him say, "I don't want to continue my relationship with you. You should stay there."

Lama Norlha waited for my response as I tilted my head and bit the side of my tongue. *I'm not giving up on Dan. I don't need another teacher. I don't care about the secrets of the Tibetans. I'm going back. Maybe Dan is just testing my commitment.*

Blinking rapidly, I attempted to waylay my tears. *Look at me, I can't even control myself for a few minutes in front of this Tibetan master.*

Lama Norlha laughed. "What this?"

"Oh Lama. My teacher in Minnesota doesn't want me to come back."

"This very good. You take empowerments. This blessing from Kalu Rinpoche very rare. You no run. No more cry."

He looked at me sternly, waved his hand, and then laughed again. "Now go. You be fine. This best."

Chapter Three
YES

I left the room and found my way to a concrete bench outside. The golden, late afternoon sun shone on the hill across the Hudson River. Silence filled the piney air. I recalled the tales of the Buddha sitting under the Bodhi tree for seven weeks until achieving enlightenment.

Lama Norlha wants me to stay? And take the empowerments only meant for retreatants? I do wish I could go into a three-year retreat.... But I can't meditate.

In my years with Dan, I'd continued attempting to meditate but could only manage about ten minutes before feeling like I was plugged into an electric socket. That is, unless I was tired. Then I fell asleep.

As I considered the possibility of participating in a retreat, I imagined sitting unmoving, my spine straight like an arrow, until bliss engulfed me. *Maybe I can finally, somehow, learn how to meditate.*

Pondering Lama Norlha's offer, I reviewed the events of the past weeks, the experiences of peace and belonging ... and of being an incapable, dense outsider. Puzzling contradictions. Beliefs and teachings that were far outside the rational. My thoughts first drifted to the afternoon Kalu Rinpoche arrived.

The monks and nuns, wrapped in burgundy robes with freshly shaved heads, had gathered along with a handful of outsiders. We all waited under the burgundy portico in front of the pastel yellow house. The leaves on the surrounding trees held droplets of moisture from a misty rain cooling the summer air. Lama smiled at the monks and nuns standing next to him. "Rain so auspicious. Local deities happy Rinpoche coming here."

If anyone looked closely, they might have seen the slightest lift to my eyebrows. *Does Lama Norlha really believe that Kalu Rinpoche's arrival and sprites or fairies are impacting the weather?*

As a kid in Sunday school, I learned how Jesus walked right out on top of some choppy water, transformed water into wine at a wedding feast, and magically multiplied a few loaves of bread and a couple of fish into enough food for the massive crowd assembled to hear him. Back then, I didn't question the veracity of those stories. But in time I'd concluded those Bible stories were folktales, parables, myths.

The monks and nuns watched the long gravel driveway, faces relaxed, eyes shining, patient even in this anticipatory waiting. No chatting, no shifting from foot to foot, no checking of watches, just an occasional glance from person to person. Observing the faces of stillness, I took a deep breath rather than emit the sigh that wanted to emerge. *How long are we going to have to wait here?*

Finally, a growing rumble of tires on gravel preceded the appearance of a shiny black sedan. After the car stopped, Kalu Rinpoche, from the backseat window, turned to look at us with an otherworldly wide-eyed innocence. His skull was shaped like an egg on its side. He looked like E.T.

Lama Norlha stepped forward to open the car door and held out his hands. Kalu Rinpoche reached back with long delicate fingers. At eighty-one years, Kalu Rinpoche was anciently serene. He stepped from the car like a delicate doe and beamed at Lama in the manner of a father gazing upon his beloved, long-lost son.

Later that afternoon, the rain stopped, and several large rainbows appeared overhead. That evening after dinner, I spotted Roberta (soon to become Trinley) and asked if she'd seen anything like that before.

She nodded, "Oh yeah, that usually happens when high lamas show up–a light rain and then rainbows." She lifted her eyebrows with a shrug of her shoulders and a "who-knew?" smile, then headed up the hill toward her room in the retreat house.

Roberta allowed the possibility of local deities influencing the weather, but could I? After all, the appearance of rain and rainbows was nothing compared to Carlos Castaneda's shape-shifting dream world she and I had pondered over glasses of red wine back in Oklahoma.

The next morning at breakfast, as I cradled my warm bowl of oatmeal, my spackling mentor Dechi stepped beside me. "I don't know if you've heard, but Chögyam Trungpa Rinpoche slipped into a coma last night at his center in Vermont. We're saying prayers for him."

I hadn't heard, but remembered Chögyam Trungpa Rinpoche as the western-dressed Tibetan teacher who'd gazed at me from the photo on Dan's bookcase.

"The lamas are doing a special all-day *puja*, chanting for his recovery. Lama Norlha asked if you'll be a wisdom *dakini* for the puja."

I stared at my oatmeal, not knowing what to say. *Lama Norlha wants me to be what?*

I knew a dakini was an enlightened being of some sort. My chest puffed out–just a tiny bit.

Dechi rubbed her bald head. "Don't worry, I'll show you what to do. Good thing you're here. The women representing the dakinis of the four directions are supposed to have long hair."

I was one of only four women on the premises who had hair longer than the width of two fingers—the maximum length allowed for those holding monastic vows. My shoulder-length hair had qualified me. Still, I was going to represent a dakini. In a sacred ceremony. I imagined the fruit of this opportunity. *Maybe I'll experience a wave of grace; or maybe some kind of opening.*

Dechi instructed me to show up at the shrine room late in the afternoon. She explained that during the puja the monks and nuns would chant to bless the *tormas*, six-inch tall conical figures shaped from whole-wheat flour and butter. My task would be to carry a saucer holding a torma out of the shrine room onto the monastery grounds. Once I reached my destination, I was to toss the torma into the air, offering it to the deities.

When I slipped into the back of the shrine room, Lama was leading the chanting. The monks and nuns were seated cross-legged in rows on the floor, repeating the Tibetan liturgy, reading from pechas resting on the low benches in front of them.

Their otherworldly, deeper-than-deep voices droned on, accompanied by a pounding drumbeat emanating from a large cylindrical drum hanging in a bright red wooden frame. Lama tapped the beat with brass cymbals, then clanged rhythmically for brief intervals. Trumpet-like horns, *gyalings*, produced music reminiscent of vaguely melodic car honking mixed with the singing of elephants. Six-foot long horns, *rag-dungs*, rested on the ground, growling extended deep bass tones.

"Shrine room" in Tibetan is *lhakhang*—abode of the gods. *Lha* is deity, *khang* means home. In a church, this room would be called the sanctuary. But this room was unlike any sanctuary even a Baptist on psychedelics might imagine. I looked around, fully taking in the explosion of technicolor—fire engine red, taxicab yellow, majestic azure blue. *Thangkas*—paintings of multi-armed, multi-colored

Tibetan deities framed in red, blue, and yellow silk brocades–lined the back wall, each hanging from a red cord. I was not in Oklahoma anymore.

The shrine, a shiny red cabinet structure, filled three-quarters of the wall to my left. A triple-life-sized brass Buddha statue rested in the center of the shrine on a chest-high ledge. This golden Buddha, forever still, sat with his legs crossed, a begging bowl in his lap. His hair, painted a blue matching the deepest blue sky, was coiled in a topknot. On each side of the Buddha, three rows of red stair-step shelves held hundreds of palm-sized metal bowls made of brass, copper, bronze, and silver. These small bowls were filled with water each morning, then emptied and dried each evening. The water, I'd been told, was an offering to the deities.

About thirty minutes after I arrived in the shrine room, one of the visiting monks handed a small saucer holding a torma to each of the three other long-haired women and then to me. I was instructed to walk to the north, to the far end of the parking lot and toss the torma into the air as an offering.

I walked out of the shrine room slowly, watching each step, holding the saucer carefully. The chanting and music continued as I walked down the stairs, out the front door, and turned left, gravel crunching beneath my feet. I passed a mountain of firewood stacked next to an old barn building. Once I reached the end of the parking lot, I stood in front of a wall of wild bushes.

I'd made it.

Tossing the sacred torma into the air as reverently as possible, I made an offering to unseen deities. The torma sailed up through the warm air for just a moment before being reclaimed by gravity and plopping into the wild branches. It hung, suspended upside down, caught in the brambles.

I tried to not smile at the sight. In the late afternoon light,

I stared at a lump of dough clinging to some branches in a bush. *Shouldn't even a representative wisdom dakini be feeling something? At least a little veneration?*

Had I slipped down a rabbit hole? Or was this just another empty religious ritual, albeit part of a mystical and foreign faith tradition? Or maybe I just lacked the sensitivity to perceive the magical grace.

The next morning at the breakfast table, Lama raised his spoon with a big grin, "Chögyam Trungpa Rinpoche out of coma. Sitting up in bed last night. Asking for *momos*."

Dechi, sitting next to me, leaned over and whispered, "Momos are Tibetan dumplings. Chögyam Trungpa Rinpoche's favorite."

I took a bite of my warm oatmeal. *Chögyam Trungpa Rinpoche was lifted from his coma with some ethereal chanting?* Was it possible that even though I hadn't felt any grace from the torma hanging in the bushes, Chögyam Trungpa Rinpoche had been impacted by the ceremony performed miles away?

Later that week, over a hundred students arrived at the center for Kalu Rinpoche's public teachings of "pointing-out" instructions, direct introduction to the nature of mind. I sat in the back of the packed shrine room, doing my best not to wiggle on the chocolate brown meditation cushion. The room was full of students, who were full of devotion. I was honored to even be in the room.

The ringing of a brass dharma bell filled the air with rhythmic metallic waves. Kalu Rinpoche was seated just to the right of the triple-life-sized Buddha, on a chest-high platform covered in red, blue, and golden silk brocades. He was holding the bell's handle, tilting it back and forth with a steady rotation of his wrist. I closed my eyes, taking a deep breath of the smoky, sandalwood-incense-filled air, trying to inhale the peace riding on those waves of sound.

Opening my eyes and softening my gaze, I focused on Kalu Rinpoche. He was now holding the bell motionlessly in front of his heart. Then he gently placed it on a silk brocade covered bench directly in front of his raised platform seat. After the intensity of the waves of the bell's ringing, the silence was as still as Minnesota air in coldest winter.

I wiggled my toes so my feet wouldn't fall asleep. *This must be what it's like to be in Tibet, in a monastery, protected by the Himalayas. I must have done something right to make it into this room.* With this thought, my gaze fell to the Electrolux vacuum cleaner, with its turquoise plastic wheels, sitting on the floor directly in front of Kalu Rinpoche's throne. The dead roaches too had made it into the room.

Ever so softly, ever so gently, Kalu Rinpoche began to speak in whispered Tibetan. Closing my eyes, all thoughts of dead roaches disappeared. I was receiving my first Tibetan "pointing-out" instructions.

The interpreter translated. Kalu Rinpoche was telling us to notice our thoughts, our minds ... and to then become aware of the "who" that was observing.

I focused on my thoughts, noting how peaceful and perfect it felt to be in this room. Every tightness, doubt, and worry melted. Then as instructed, I focused on who was thinking that thought. I was aware of a "me" sitting in the room, so I again focused on who was aware of that me. And then on who was aware of the one who was aware. I could only picture an unending succession of "me's" observing me, like cascading reflections in a funhouse mirror.

Locked in my attempt to understand logically, I was no longer bathed in silent peacefulness.

I hadn't been able to grasp the point of these "pointing-out" instructions. They hadn't made any sense. And yet I remembered how something, a small still knowing, had beckoned, "Yes. Here."

In the lingering daylight, I shifted my weight on the rough concrete bench, then kicked my feet in the dirt. Cool air drifted up from the Hudson River. The windows of the houses on the hilly bank across the river now glimmered with the glow of electric lights.

Lama must have seen some quality or capacity in me, or he never would have asked me to stay to receive the empowerments for the retreat practices. Maybe I really can become a meditator. Then Dan will welcome me back. Maybe that's why he wanted me to stay here. I just need to apply myself and become the best student ever. I'll learn how to experience the "me" who is observing.

I remembered the stillness of sitting with Kalu Rinpoche. The sense of home. As my arms filled with goose bumps, I hugged them across my chest. And I knew I would stay. At least for a while.

Chapter Four
BEST STUDENT EVER

Lama Norlha's haunting melodic drone filled the shrine room as the sun emerged with its promise to warm the frosty air. He tapped a steady rhythm with brass cymbals, accompanied by the deep heartbeat of two Tibetan bass drums. The four-foot cylindrical drums rested at the ends of the monk and nun rows, one played by a monk, the other by a nun. It had been three months since Lama asked me to stay. The retreatants had begun their retreat and Kalu Rinpoche had returned to his home monastery in India.

Lama was seated on his designated floor cushion at the head of the monks' row. He was leading the first of three daily chanting sessions, pujas. The first two corresponded with sunrise and sunset. Each lasted about two hours. They included rapid chanting of a complex text accompanied by drumbeat, cymbals, bells, and horns. After dinner came the third puja, *Chenrezig*. It was shorter, simpler, and more leisurely paced. Chanting Chenrezig puja was accessible to anyone. The pecha for this third puja had an English transliteration for the Tibetan letters (which appeared as hieroglyphics to me), as well as an English translation.

During my first few weeks after deciding to stay, in addition to chanting Chenrezig puja each day, I attempted to join in the chanting of the two longer pujas. The pechas used by the monks and nuns for these two longer pujas didn't have a transliteration or a translation, but I found copies of both pechas with transliterations—*Om nang shi nam dak rang shin lhun drup pay.*

Since I was the first in line to prepare for the next retreat, I claimed the cushion at the head of the row directly behind the one reserved for nuns. Even though I was the only one in line, I concluded I deserved the spot.

The chanting was like Tibetan speed rap. At times, the words blurred into a hum. The explanation for this speed: more repetitions, more accumulated merit. I wondered if all this "more" really was better, but who was I to question? These rituals were centuries old. But even with the transliteration, I could just barely follow the syllables with my eyes—every now and then I could join in for a phrase or two.

Lama Norlha was a traditionalist, so wanted us to read the Tibetan script, not the transliteration. He cited a power, a blessing, and a transmission in not only repeating the Tibetan words, but also in viewing the squiggly Tibetan letters. After I'd struggled to chant with the transliteration for several weeks, Lama suggested I use the two longer puja sessions to begin the first of the preliminary practices—*Ngöndro*, prostrations.

"Prostrations difficult. You do during chanting time. Only chant Chenrezig puja. First finish prostrations. This very auspicious."

So, now during both the sunrise and sunset pujas I was performing prostrations. Standing in the back of the room with my palms together, I touched the top of my head, my throat, then my heart—symbolically offering up my body, speech, and mind. Next, bending at my waist, I placed my hands in front of my feet, dropped to my knees, and slid my hands forward until I was flat on the ground. Face down. Body in full surrender. Prostrate. Finally, I pushed myself back up to a kneeling position, then stood to begin again.

Completing the four Ngöndro practices (literally translated as "going before" practices) is a prerequisite to entering three-year retreat. Each part of Ngöndro builds upon the previous.

1. First, prostrations begin the ongoing process of surrender, a flattening of pride. They're intended to connect the student with the Buddha, with his teachings, with the entire lineage.
2. The second practice is repeating Dorje Sempa's hundred-syllable mantra. This purifies, removing obscurations.
3. Mandala offerings are the third installment. Performing this practice, the student accumulates merit and wisdom.
4. Finally, in the practice of Guru Yoga, the student begins to unite mentally with the wisdom mind of the teacher and of all the Buddhas.

Traditionally, each of the four Ngöndro segments is repeated 100,000 times. An extra 11,111 are added to the requirements to make up for any potential errors. So, I was first working on completing 111,111 prostrations. I took comfort in the fact that no one was expected to perform every repetition perfectly. I knew if I practiced diligently, during both the morning and pre-dinner puja sessions, it would take about six months to complete the 111,111. Six months of intense physical training. Buddhist boot camp.

Starting prostrations was like becoming a part of a special club. Tips and tricks were shared. First, I was directed to purchase a prostration board. In Tibet, a plank of wood was used, or maybe just the floor, or the ground. But here, lightweight particleboard had been found to be ideal. So, I visited a nearby hardware store and had a piece of caramel-brown composite wood cut down to forty inches by six feet.

As advised, I also purchased a metal tub of paste wax, then

applied it to the smooth side of the particle board, shining it with a rag to achieve a glossy, slick, finish–for better sliding. Finally, I cut beige carpet scraps into two hand-sized pieces for placing beneath my palms, so I could slide ever more quickly to the face-flat-on-the-ground surrendered position.

Traditionally repetitions are tracked with a beaded mala. The beads are made of wood, like rosewood or sandalwood, or of large round seeds, or even precious stones. They're strung just loosely enough on a cord to allow the thumb to move one bead at a time while holding the gap in the cord between the thumb and forefinger.

At the small monastery store, I purchased a mahogany brown rosewood mala to keep count. But as I slid to the floor and back up again, the 108 beads kept swinging in my hand, smacking me in the face. So, I tried using a handheld metal clicking counter, the kind used to tally people entering a stadium. I placed the metal on the floor at the top of my prostration board, clicking with my outstretched hands each time I was flat on my belly.

Perhaps because that click, click, click was a distraction during the chanting, someone suggested I try using a mala with fewer beads. So, I purchased a sandalwood mala with smaller aromatic beads, then strung thirty-six of the beads onto a piece of thin purple satin ribbon. Not only was it beautiful, it worked perfectly. Three times around was 108.

I was sore at first, performing these Tibetan-style burpees for hours each day, but after a couple of weeks I became expert at sliding face down on my prostration board, then pushing myself back up to standing. It was physically demanding. But this was a meditation practice I could do.

Performing prostrations is not just about meeting the physical challenge. After all, it's a meditation. The physical exertion is combined with repeating a prayer while imagining a complex visualization in the mind's eye, creating an alternative reality. For the prostration visualization, first there's a wish-fulfilling tree. Mine was a sturdy oak with bright green leaves. In the center of the tree, one's root guru–for me, Kalu Rinpoche–rests in the form of the sapphire-blue primordial Buddha, Vajradhara, surrounded by all the past teachers of the lineage (beginning with the historical Buddha) as well as by both wrathful and peaceful deities with their retinues.

Next, I was to imagine my mother on my left and my father on my right, behind me the rest of my relatives, along with all beings in the universe. In front, my enemies. All of us–friends, family, acquaintances, enemies, every living being–prostrating to this magical tree filled with wisdom beings. Since I couldn't actually manage to visualize all the complicated details, I focused on Kalu Rinpoche as Vajradhara, resting in the center of the magical oak tree filled with loving helpers.

As my body became more and more accustomed to the strenuous down-on-the-ground-and-up-again movement, I repeated the refuge prayer in Tibetan, gradually connecting meaning to the Tibetan words.

palden lama dampa namla kyab su chio
yidam kyil khor gyi lha tsok namla kyab su chio
sangye chom dende namla kyab su chio
dam pay chö namla kyab su chio
pakpay gendün namla kyab su chio
pawo khandro chö kyong sung may tsok
yeshe chi chen dang denpa namla kyab su chio

I take refuge in the glorious holy lamas, the kind root lama, and the lineage masters.
I take refuge in all the yidams and deities gathered in the mandala.
I take refuge in all the Buddhas.

I take refuge in all the holy dharma.
I take refuge in all the noble sangha.
I take refuge in the assembly of the dakas, dakinis, and dharmapalas
Those who have the all-seeing eye of wisdom.

Beginning these Ngöndro practices, I was following the lineage of enlightened Buddhist masters. Many of the visualized deities originated in the native shamanistic Bön religion long before Buddhism came to Tibet. I didn't have difficulty with the refuge tree's peaceful deities, but the wrathful ones, the ones surrounded by fire, with bared teeth, weapons dripping blood, and necklaces of skulls, conjured echoes of Baptist fire-and-brimstone. But when these waves of reservation arose, I dismissed them by focusing on the promised reward of enlightenment.

In addition to beginning Ngöndro, I started learning the language, so I could chant and understand the pujas and practice liturgies. Plus, I began working toward saving thirteen thousand dollars–twelve thousand for the retreat tuition fees and one thousand to cover personal supplies during the three years of retreat.

Shortly after I'd arrived, Trinley confided how grateful she was that Lama had invited her to participate in the retreat free of charge. However, when I inquired about the possibility of also receiving a scholarship, even a partial one, I was told that the monastery couldn't afford to support those taking part in a retreat. I told myself that Trinley deserved her special dispensation. After all, she had a natural capacity for meditation. Plus, she'd been living and studying with the Tibetans while I'd been in Minnesota with Dan. Still, I silently bristled.

Struggling to find an antidote to my jealous disappointment, I called on Jesus's parable of the prodigal son. When the younger of two brothers returned home after many years, having squandered his inheritance, his father joyfully welcomed the wayward son back in celebration. But the older, dutiful son was unable to recognize he'd lost nothing–unable to appreciate his father's relief and delight with the return of his lost son.

Not wanting to emulate that envious older son, I corralled my thoughts into the most positive lane I could find. *Earning this money is how I'm supporting everyone here at the monastery, the monks and nuns ... and Lama. Besides, finding work was easy.*

Prior to the retreat, Trinley had been cleaning several nearby houses to earn enough to cover the costs of the personal items and supplies she'd need during her three years locked away from the world. When she entered the retreat, I took over those jobs. Then I placed an ad in a local paper to find a few more. My room and board fees were only two-hundred and fifty dollars per month, but I needed thirteen thousand dollars to participate in the next retreat. So, most mornings after prostrations and breakfast, I headed out to vacuum, dust, and mop.

When I decided to stay at the monastery, I upped my status from visitor to resident, so no longer had to sleep in the women's dorm bunk bed in the main house. I was assigned my own room in the building just next to the clump of bushes where I'd thrown the torma. This building, nicknamed "the barn," had housed machinery in a previous incarnation, but had been converted into a two-story, six-room house–three small rooms upstairs, and three down. Its nickname was well-deserved. Gaps between the first floor's weathered wooden floorboards offered glimpses of the dirt below. The only source of heat was a woodstove under the staircase. The nearest running water or bathroom was over two hundred steps away in the main house.

My middle room on the ground level was the smallest of the six. I would have preferred an upstairs carpeted room, or at least one of the slightly larger ones on the ground floor, but suspected

Lama must have noticed my flares of pride and was trying to teach me humility. Still, I was grateful for the quiet privacy.

My fantasy of returning to Minnesota and Dan, although still present, was increasingly preempted by the possibility of actually making it into a three-year retreat ... and becoming enlightened. I planned to become the best student ever. To achieve star student status. Maybe even become Lama's favorite–my go-to strategy for receiving the acceptance I so craved. The tendrils of this well-established tactic had been vining for years.

Chapter Five
PLANTING THE SEED

On my way to third grade class at William McKinley Elementary in Enid, Oklahoma, I gingerly avoided the cracks in the sidewalk while chanting to myself, "Step on a crack; break your mother's back." The stained concrete was splintered by the roots of the row of elms stretching ahead in a line as far as I could see. I suspected all this crack avoidance was probably silly–how could a misstep harm my mother? Still, I didn't want to take any chances. I certainly didn't want to disappoint her. I wanted her love.

She grew up in a tiny Texas town. When she was seven, she glanced down the grocery store aisle and spotted her mother, a high school teacher, picking up a package of baloney and sliding it into her handbag. Seeing this unthinkable act, my mother slipped out to sit in the hot, humid car to wait. She never spoke of it to her mother.

This stealing was something her mother continued to do. Did the shop owners know? A daunting presence at three hundred pounds, my grandmother righteously claimed whatever she wanted. She was so all-pervasive, so unboundaried, that my mother learned to shield herself in an impenetrable bubble. My mother avoided the intensity of too much connection while I yearned for more.

Sometimes, in a flight of fantasy, I imagine sitting and talking with her before incarnating into this life, sharing coffee or a glass of wine, choosing the roles we'd play to perfectly create the experiences needed for surrender, for opening. Buddhists view life's circumstances as the consequences of our previous actions–*karma*. Like when a billiard cue ball hits the waiting triangular rack and the balls fly into precise actions based on the nature of the hit–some balls ping recklessly off the side of the green felt, while others fall gently to rest in a pocket. From Baptist teachings, I'd learned about original sin, original karma–the consequences of Adam and Eve's disobedience. The snake tempted Eve, then Eve convinced Adam to eat the fruit of the tree of the knowledge of good and evil. With this awareness, opposites–this and that–were born. From then on, banished from the garden, we've been wandering in this world of duality, separate from God–longing to reconnect.

My life began as an accident. I was conceived, out of wedlock, in the late summer after my parents' freshman year of college. They were high school sweethearts. She'd been the valedictorian before they attended the University of Texas. I wonder so many things. Did it happen in the back seat of my father's car? Did my mother tell her parents she was pregnant prior to the wedding? What kind of ceremony did they have? Did they even have a ceremony? It was never discussed. I never asked.

The sky-reaching elms that shaded my walk to my third-grade classroom, their roots sunk deep into the earth, would all be gone to Dutch elm disease before I finished high school. Yet within me, a lifetime of seeking loving acceptance had taken root. Although I was ashamed of it and tried to hide it, I longed to find some way, somehow, somewhere I could rest like a baby in my mother's arms, safely cradled, free from all want and danger. I wanted that kind of peace. That kind of "I love you." I looked for this home in the eyes of my grade-school teachers. And from Jesus–at Enid, Oklahoma's First Baptist Church.

My memories of that First Baptist Church are a collage of every experience of church, every preacher, every sermon. I peer down a long alleyway of recollections, through the eyes of a wide-eyed, awestruck girl.

One Sunday morning when I was eight, I'd strolled the few blocks to church alone and slipped into the sanctuary, surrounded by strangers. I don't know why I was there without my parents. Maybe that Sunday my mother was caring for our new baby brother, my father away on another of his business trips.

Scooting into one of the wooden pews, I was held by the rich warmth of the caramel-colored wood. A life-sized wooden carving of Jesus nailed to the cross filled the wall directly behind the pulpit. Above Jesus, a large glass window was covered by a red velvet curtain. Behind the curtain, behind the glass, a neck-deep tub of water waited for those who were called to be baptized, saved from eternal hell and damnation. The curtain would then be opened and the repentee, dressed only in a thick white cotton baptismal robe, would join the preacher man in the tank of holy water. With the words "I baptize you in the name of the Father, the Son, and the Holy Spirit," the preacher ceremoniously tilted the saved-from-hell sinner backward under the water.

Sitting in the sanctuary, hearing the swelling chords from the organ, I imagined the beams of the ceiling opening into heaven, angels dissolving the roof. I was washed in sweetness, floating free from the heavy pull of gravity. My eight-year-old senses perceived a rarefied, embracing stillness I couldn't understand, name, or comprehend.

At the end of the service, the preacher proclaimed how Jesus had suffered on the cross so I could be forgiven for my sins. "Come, come now, come forward, come to Jesus." His voice boomed the invitation again and again as the pipe organ's notes filled the vaulted ceiling. I wasn't sure exactly what my sins were, but I was pretty sure I had some. And maybe they were bad enough to send me to hell. But, most of all, I wanted to belong, to be embraced–like those children in the Bible story who were welcomed into Jesus's lap.

As terrified as I was of walking down the long aisle, of being viewed by all those strangers, the sound of the resounding melody and the calling from the preacher-man became the outstretched hand of Jesus. Jesus, with his long wavy hair, kind brown eyes, a glowing halo, was reaching out to me.

In a boldly uncharacteristic moment, I stood up and stepped into the aisle. Then it was too late to turn back. All I could do was walk toward the front of the church. It took about twenty steps to reach the grinning preacher who took my hand, then asked my name. So many eyes were staring at me. The promise of heaven vanished. I did not find Jesus–just an ordinary sweaty man with a pasted-on smile.

The next week, my mother accompanied me to the Wednesday night baptismal service. I was dunked in the tub of water above the altar. Afterwards, only a pile of dry folded clothing and a thin terry towel waited for me in the musty changing room. By the end of that year our family was no longer attending the First Baptist Church.

Chapter Six
PROSTRATION OLYMPICS

I was performing prostrations in the back of the shrine room unable to maintain focus on the mantra and visualization. Instead, I kept peeking over at a newcomer to the monastery—Willa. Out of the corner of my eye, I could see her sitting in the spot I'd previously claimed, behind the nuns' row headed by Dechi, my spackling mentor.

After four months of again and again and again sliding to the ground and then back to standing during both the sunrise and sunset pujas, I'd begun to feel a part of monastery life. The physical effort and mantra prayer chanting felt soothing, despite my limited success with the complex visualization of the refuge tree. But this morning I couldn't find any kind of comfort in my practice. As I pushed myself up to a standing position, I couldn't stop my eyes from wandering in Willa's direction. She was sitting perfectly erect, reading the Tibetan pecha—not the transliterated version—and was even able to join in on some phrases.

Was Lama glancing in her direction and smiling? This twenty-year-old student from nearby Vassar College, with her cascade of wavy shoulder-length auburn hair and ivory complexion, had spent a semester in Nepal living with a Tibetan family where she became proficient in the language. Just several weeks earlier, when she first visited, she was seated next to Lama at lunch, and they chatted in Tibetan. Occasionally I caught a recognizable word or two from the far end of the table. Soon after, she moved into the empty room next to mine on the first floor of the barn. Lama had invited her to stay at the monastery and participate in the daily chanting while she completed her college courses.

This morning, as usual, I'd pulled myself out of bed and stumbled across the parking lot in the softness of the pre-dawn light. My eyes were barely open as I climbed the stairs of the main house to the shrine room. Earlier, long before any appearance of daylight, I'd been awakened by some movement in the room next to mine. I checked the time–a few minutes before four. When I entered the shrine room, Willa was picking up her prostration board from the floor and leaning it next to mine against the back wall before finding her seat for chanting. She'd been practicing for two hours before I even managed to get out of bed. My hoped-for status as best student was in serious jeopardy.

Willa continued rising before four each morning to perform her prostration practice. And I continued my routine–cleaning houses during the day, prostrating each morning and each evening during puja. If anyone had asked, I would have denied my festering imperative to complete my 111,111 prostrations before Willa finished hers. Attempting to withdraw from my clandestine prostration race, I called on the Middle Ages proverb "Comparisons are odious." I was certain my incessant competitive thoughts were undesirable, certainly not holy, and clearly incompatible with enlightenment. I recalled Dan's lesson from the gnostic teacher Vitvan, "No matter what anyone does, no matter what anyone says, it has no value until you place value on it." It didn't help. I couldn't seem to find a way to resign from my secret prostration Olympics.

Several months after Willa arrived, her favorite grandmother died. And then, at Christmas time, just as she was finishing her final semester at Vassar, her mom's heart suddenly stopped and she died on the sidewalk in front of a store in Berkeley. When Willa returned from her trip to California for the funeral, she was no longer interested in finishing her degree. She only wanted to practice. But Lama insisted she complete her classwork and final papers needed for graduation.

I never saw Willa cry. But at night, through the thin wall of her room next to mine, I could hear her sobbing as she read the *Bardo Thodul*, the *Tibetan Book of the Dead*, aloud in English for her mother. She was grieving, yet remained focused on her practices. I chafed at my inability to find some way to control my swells of comparison and competition with this motherless child.

After I'd completed over fifty thousand prostrations, after months of sliding flat on the ground and pushing myself back to standing position, a teacher from Tibet came to our center for a visit. As I was headed to the sink to wash my soup bowl after dinner, he stopped me, smiling. No one else was around.

In his halting English, he said, "You doing good, prostrations."

"Yes, it's taking me a long time. I wish I could get finished faster," I didn't speak my next thought–*before Willa.*

"You can," he smiled.

I thought I was going to learn some insider technique–a Tibetan prostration secret.

His eyes gleamed as he transmitted his gem of information. "Speed up."

I nodded and thanked him.

How I wished I could comply. I imagined Willa sliding up and down her prostration board, gliding like a gazelle. But I was working as hard as I could. I was never much of an athlete, but this practice was making me stronger, and not just physically. The muscles in my arms and back began to show definition, like a bodybuilder. I was also gaining the capacity to remain focused on the visualization. However, my knees were suffering. Even though I was kneeling on a rectangular piece of two-inch-thick high-density foam, my knees began to ache constantly from the recurring motion and pounding. After thousands of prostrations, after the beige carpet scraps were indented with my handprints, my foam kneepad cushion began to disintegrate, so I purchased the first of several replacements.

Worried I was causing permanent injury to my knees, I decided I needed to check in with Lama. Standing in his doorway, I waited for him to look up from his pechas.

"Lama, I'm afraid I'm damaging my knees."

"No problem. No think that. Just do prostrations. You be fine."

So, I did. Day after day. Month after month. Twice a day for almost two hours each session. Down on the ground and back up again. Chanting the refuge prayer. Visualizing the refuge tree. Allowing myself to rest in the shelter of Kalu Rinpoche's presence. But my knees constantly ached. Climbing and descending the stairs was painful. I had to press against the sides of the toilet stall to lower myself onto the seat.

One evening at dinner, an older visiting Tibetan teacher was discussing his knee pain. I stopped eating my yogurt so I wouldn't miss his explanation of the cause. He confessed that as a young monk he'd stepped over a pecha bench filled with Tibetan liturgy books. He was certain this lack of respect for the teachings was the source of his recurrent pain. I wasn't so sure. I imagined a piece or two of high-density foam would have been helpful.

Completing the 111,111 prostrations seemed an unending task. Each day was the same, one after another, requiring more effort, focus, and discipline than anything I'd ever attempted. At times I wondered how I could possibly endure another moment of the dull tedium. But this flatness was woven with unexpected moments of quiet contentment. It's said that one prostration, done properly, done fully, is enough. But then, I haven't heard of anyone being credited with doing that one perfect prostration.

Finally, after a little more than six months of daily effort, I completed prostration number 111,111. Before Willa. The next day, when I visited Lama's room to tell him what I'd accomplished, I summoned my best acting chops to disguise my pride and appear humble. I was certain he'd give me some kind of commendation, along with private instructions on the second Ngöndro practice–visualizing the deity of purification, pearlescent Dorje Sempa, and repeating his hundred-syllable mantra.

"Lama, I finished my prostrations."

"This very good. Now you start again."

What? Begin again? Completing the prostrations was one of the most difficult things I'd ever done, more difficult than leaving the nest of my marriage. *Did I do something wrong? Can he see my pride?*

"But, but Lama," I stuttered. "What about starting Dorje Sempa practice?"

"Yes, you start. Also, you making 108 prostrations every day. This very auspicious. So good."

"Okay." I did my best to appear surrendered and compliant. "And what about puja? I'm pretty sure I can chant now without using the transliteration."

I held my breath, hoping he'd approve.

"Yes, you chanting now. Very good."

I backed out of the room, nodding with a pasted-on smile, then padded down the hallway toward the shrine room to retrieve my prostration board. As I carried it across the parking lot toward my room, I wrestled with Lama's directive. *Do I really have to do more prostrations? Every day? That's going to take away from the time I can spend on my Dorje Sempa practice. But I have to comply. It was an instruction from my lama. Well, he said it would be good for me. Maybe it will be. It could keep me strong for retreat. But what about my knees?*

The next evening, I laid my prostration board on the empty floor space in front of my wooden cot-sized bed. It just fit. And did 108 prostrations. Then sitting cross-legged on my bed, I copied Dorje Sempa's one hundred syllable mantra onto a white index card.

om bed zra sa to sa ma ya
ma nu pa la ya
bed zra sa to te no pa
ti ta dri do me ba wa
su to koy yo me ba wa
su po koy o me ba wa
a nu ra to me ba wa
sar wa sid dim me pra yat sa
sar wa kar ma su tsa me
tsi tang shi ri ya ku ru hung
ha ha ha ha ho ban ga wen
sar wa ta ta ga ta
bed zra ma me mun tsa
bed zri ba wa ma ha
sa ma ya sa to ah

I counted the syllables. One hundred and three. I wondered if anyone else had noticed the imprecision. But then, I didn't know how to read Sanskrit–maybe a couple of the transliterated syllables were merged in the ancient tongue. I understood that the mantra didn't have a translation–that its transformative power comes from the vibration, the sound of the Sanskrit syllables.

Before I could start accumulating my Dorje Sempa mantra repetitions, I needed to memorize all those syllables. While cleaning a house–wiping blue glass cleaner from a bathroom mirror, scrubbing grease splatter from a stovetop, or pushing a vacuum around a living room carpet–I repeated longer and longer segments. I checked my three-by-five card , adding one line at a time. My skill at memorization, honed during my years of performing, was coming in handy. After two days, I could repeat the entire mantra without pulling the card from my pocket.

Based on my previous unsuccessful attempts at meditation, I'd worried I'd find it difficult to simply sit and chant. But surprisingly, something had shifted while doing all those prostrations. I found I could remain seated for an hour or two at a time while I quietly vocalized the syllables of Dorje Sempa's mantra. As I chanted, I visualized his milky-white body hanging out above my head, his purifying nectar pouring from his body through his big toe into me. The visualization of Dorje Sempa resting on a moon disc held by a lotus was far less complex than the myriad elements of the prostration practice's refuge tree. I pictured Dorje Sempa showing up like a rainbow, or a hologram—a representation of the union of emptiness and form.

Of course, my attention wandered. But there were also stretches of relaxation, of being bathed in compassionate grace, soothed by the hum of my repetitions of the mantra. At times, I opened my eyes and stared at Dorje Sempa's image, a five-by-seven print resting on my little altar. I'd propped the picture behind my set of seven brass bowls, lined up like the bowls on Lama's dresser, and like the hundreds in the shrine room.

Within a month of beginning my Dorje Sempa practice, I stopped doing that extra round of 108 prostrations. I didn't consult Lama on my decision, rationalizing that I wasn't technically disobeying—just delaying. I planned to resume just as soon as I finished my Ngöndro practices. But first, I needed to focus on accumulating the 111,111 repetitions of Dorje Sempa's mantra.

I quickly realized this practice was going to take longer to complete than prostrations. It had taken about twenty minutes to finish one round of 108 prostrations, but repeating Dorje Sempa's mantra required over thirty minutes per round. This fact contributed to my decision to delay that second set of prostrations. Yet even though I was aware of my increasing focus and calm, I could not seem to end my secret competition with Willa. I so wanted to find a way to stop my odious comparing, so I decided to seek Lama's help.

One evening after Chenrezig puja, I followed Lama to his room. Once he climbed into his yellow padded meditation box, I lowered myself to his floor.

"Lama, I can't seem to find a way to stop competing with Willa. I keep comparing myself to her. I feel like she's so much better than me."

He peered at me over his reading glasses, "This good. You trying harder to be more like Willa. She has qualities, best qualities."

He focused on his pechas and quietly began chanting, not looking up again. I waited. When I realized he wasn't going to say anything else, I got up and backed out of the room as I'd learned to do, careful not to turn my back on him.

Plodding across the parking lot, I shook my head in a silent gesture of no. *I don't know how I can possibly try harder to be more like Willa. Besides, how will trying harder help? If only I could talk with Kalu Rinpoche. He wouldn't even have to say anything. Just being in his presence would make everything clear.*

In the meantime, I decided simply to continue my practice. To never give up.

Chapter Seven
THINK LIKE A TIBETAN

While working on first completing prostrations and then on repeating Dorje Sempa's mantra, I was also learning to read, write, and speak Tibetan. Dechi was my first tutor. When I didn't have a cleaning job in the afternoon or on weekends, we'd meet in the dining hall.

Dechi began by introducing the thirty consonants and four vowels. Once I could read each letter, I began forming syllables using the same technique employed to teach young monks to read in Tibet. I'd sing each letter one by one, then the full syllable. As the sun reached through the dining room windows overlooking the Hudson, my voice echoed in the vastness of the room, filled with enough plastic-tablecloth-covered tables to seat over a hundred people. I felt like a kindergartener. But soon, I was able to combine those syllables into words.

I was also learning to write the Tibetan script. In elementary school, I practiced with my fat red pencil, dragging the lead across the sweet rag paper lined with alternating ocean-blue solid and dotted lines. Now, each evening in my room, I used a calligraphy pen to copy the text of the Chenrezig puja onto the pristine white pages in my spiral-bound notebook.

After I could read a few phrases, I graduated from Dechi's tutelage to Drupten's. It was one thing to be able to form words, even write them, but quite another to understand their meaning.

Drupten, a western monk in his thirties with an aquiline nose and twinkling eyes, had studied with Lama Norlha since Lama first arrived in this country. He was a graduate of the first retreat and currently Lama's translator, a position he inherited from Yeshe, another western monk. Now in his second retreat, Yeshe was such a stellar student of the Tibetan language that after his first retreat, he served as Kalu Rinpoche's translator. When Yeshe took his vows and became a monk, Kalu Rinpoche named him Yeshe Gyamtso, Ocean of Wisdom.

Unlike Yeshe, I didn't possess an ocean of wisdom when it came to learning the Tibetan language. After twice flunking Spanish in high school, I managed to avoid studying any foreign language. Thankfully, my lack of capacity for learning languages didn't seem to bother Drupten. He smiled at my blank looks as I stared at the Tibetan text, willing myself to remember.

After I completed my 111,111 prostrations and could join the chanting during the two longer pujas each day, I had a chance to test-drive my developing reading skills. At first, I could only follow along with my eyes. But soon I was chanting phrases and then entire sections. Although my understanding of the words was spotty, I could ride the waves of the non-Western melodies, like I had as a child listening to musical theater showtunes on the record player's spinning black discs. And as meanings of the chanted Tibetan came into focus, I began to discern the basic structural pattern of each practice.

First, the deity or deities are visualized–brought into form. Then, for most of the practices, one imagines oneself as the deity. The chanted text describes intricate details of the deity's appearance, their retinues, and their compassionate activities. In some of the more advanced liturgies, the practitioner embodies a *yab-yum* manifestation, a deity and consort in sexual embrace. At the end of each liturgy, the visualization dissolves into emptiness and the practitioner rests in stillness. Over the past centuries, these virtual worlds have been chanted into existence and then dissolved hundreds of thousands of times.

Even though it was challenging to keep up with the chanting during the longer sunrise and sunset pujas, and although I struggled to get out of bed in time for morning puja, I was drawn to our group chanting times. Together we were creating make-believe worlds, like the fairytales of my youth. Or like in grade school, when I checked out every *Nancy Drew* book from the library, then snuggled in the corner of the living room, turning the well-worn pages, transforming myself into bold and intrepid Nancy. Or like when creating a character for performing.

The morning puja included repeating the Twenty-One Praises to Tara, the mother of the Buddhas, a green-skinned, feminine manifestation of compassion. As I repeated Tara's Twenty-One Praises and her mantra, I bathed in motherly acceptance. The sunset puja focused on Mahakala–black in color, with four arms, three eyes surrounded by flames, and standing in the midst of a mountain of fire–a wrathful aspect of compassion. But my favorite chanting session was the third of the day, after dinner–Chenrezig practice. Since the pace was much slower, I could actually chant every word. And with daily repetition, I soon memorized the entire liturgy. With eyes closed, I imagined myself as pure white light appearing as the lovingly compassionate Chenrezig, sitting on a lotus held by a moon disc.

Four-armed Chenrezig is the archetypal representation of a *bodhisattva*–one who has compassionately vowed not to pass out of cyclic existence into *nirvana* until every other being has transcended; to be the last to go, to allow every other sentient being to go first. His body radiates five colors of wisdom light with the power to transform the sufferings of all sentient beings. His first two hands meet at the heart, holding a wish-fulfilling jewel. His right lower hand clasps a crystal mala, the lower left hand, a white lotus flower.

As my capacity with the Tibetan language improved, I became curious about some of the problem-causing, mischievous, troll-like entities mentioned in the sunset puja. One evening, as we filed out of the shrine room, I stopped Lama to ask for an explanation. He turned toward me, "This not something you need understand. Leave alone. No make difficult. In Tibet, demons on the outside causing trouble. In America, demons inside–in your mind."

After he left the room, I paused to survey the glistening domes of the rows and rows of water bowls resting upside down. During our chanting they'd been emptied and dried. In the morning, during puja, they'd be refilled. *For Lama, for the Tibetans, demons actually exist. But Lama advised I not think like a Tibetan. At least not about this.*

My emotions and thoughts were certainly troublesome, even out of control, but I'd never thought of them as demons. To me, demons were fictional beings appearing in books or horror movies, like *The Exorcist.* They never had any kind of external reality.

As I headed down the stairs for dinner, I imagined my neurotic tendencies lurking in the shadows. At the bottom of the stairs, I slipped on my shoes, noting the gentle hum of conversation wafting down the hallway from the dining room.

My paradigm of reality, a view I'd not previously questioned, was based on the scientific discoveries of Plato, Aristotle, Galileo, and Newton, and more recently Einstein, Heisenberg, and Bohr. These scientifically based certainties were woven with psychological models born of the concepts of Freud and Jung. But the Tibetan mind, with a language emerging from Sanskrit rather than Latin, perceives reality through a different collective paradigm–like the fresh display in a kaleidoscope after the slightest turn of the lens. The configuration changes, even though the raw elements creating the pattern remain the same.

When I reached the dining room, I retrieved my yellow plastic bowl from its designated spot in the cabinet below the ledge separating the kitchen from the dining room. As I filled my dish with beef and pasta soup, almost-forgotten tales of Jesus casting out demons drifted into awareness. I remembered the story of Legion. He lived among tombs, cut himself with stones, and couldn't be kept in captivity. Jesus sent Legion's demons into a herd of wild pigs, then the pigs, in a frenzy, rushed off a cliff into the sea and drowned. We'd probably classify Legion as a schizophrenic. But for those in the ancient biblical world, Legion was possessed by a multitude of demons.

I'd adjusted my thinking to allow for the seemingly inconsistent application of the rules and vows. The monks and nuns had taken vows to not kill, yet meat was regularly consumed–but only the meat from large animals. I reasoned that in Tibet, the yak was an important source of sustenance, like the buffalo had been for this country's original inhabitants. Here, the monks and nuns were allowed to eat meat from cows–but not from chickens or fish. And eating beef didn't technically break the no-killing vow because the cows were already dead in their pristine cellophane-covered packages from the refrigerated cases of the local supermarket. However, I struggled with the logic forbidding the eating of eggs. Even unfertilized eggs were off limits because eggs hold the potential for life.

After I'd taken vows as a nun, I was given the honor of cooking breakfast for a visiting Rinpoche. To my surprise, I was informed that he wanted scrambled eggs. Because of my vows, Lama arranged for someone else to crack the eggs into a bowl. But I was allowed to whisk them and pour them into the frying pan.

In my more pensive moments, I hoped all my rationalizing (including my decision to delay doing more prostrations) wasn't unreasonable. I didn't want to emulate my grandmother's capacity for justification. But I reassured myself by recalling that these Buddhist teachings had passed from enlightened master to enlightened master in an unbroken lineage for thousands of years.

The Buddha is said to have presented eighty-four thousand different teachings, each tailored to the capacity of the student. Tibetan Buddhism speaks of three basic levels of the teachings–the *Hinayana*, the *Mahayana*, and the *Vajrayana*. *Yana* is translated as vehicle, or path, or way. A restriction at one level might not be applied in the same way in the next. That seemed reasonable enough. After all, a young child is forbidden to cross the street alone, but in time gains the awareness and capacity to be able to look both ways before venturing forth.

The Hinayana, translated as the "narrow way," provides the foundation of rules meant to help us live together, to create order and the possibility of a harmonious society. These restrictions are likened to the blinders on a horse–a support, like the Ten Commandments. The Hinayana view is like peering into the kaleidoscope of reality with a fixed dial, stable and protected by agreed-upon norms and guardrails.

The Mahayana, translated as the "great way," rests on the structure and order of the Hinayana. The Mahayana is the way of loving kindness, of the bodhisattva, of Chenrezig. At the level of the Mahayana teachings, one begins to develop enough maturity–enough stability–to act (or abstain from action) with skillful means, with discernment arising from compassion rather than by simply staying inside the parameters of rules and regulations.

I found reason here as well. Lama ordered the roach extermination to protect the health of his beloved Kalu Rinpoche. I remembered Jesus's Bodhisattva guidance, "Do unto others as you would have them do unto you." And I recalled how Jesus demonstrated Bodhisattva compassion by disobeying the restrictions of the Sabbath to perform compassionate acts of healing.

Hinayana discipline supports the awakening of Mahayana compassion. By carrying spiders outside rather than stepping on them, I practiced abstaining from killing. And even though I couldn't bring myself to allow the mosquitoes to drink their fill of my blood, I used a puff of breath to send them away. These small actions started to transform my previously unrecognized subtle aggression into a new warmth of tender caring. Mahayana compassion begins with developing compassion for a separate other. Ultimately the appearance of separation begins to dissolve. In the Vajrayana teachings, every experience, every thought, every feeling, you and me–all are arisings of empty, luminous, radiant potentiality.

The Vajrayana, translated as Diamond Vehicle, likens the fundamental nature of perceived reality to the child of a barren woman, a mirage, a dream–like the empty grid of potentiality revealed in Star Trek's virtual reality holodeck. When the Star Trek crew member declares, "Computer, end program," the holographic fantasy world disappears, even though everything appeared to be so solidly real just moments earlier. The deity visualization practices–creating an alternative reality then dissolving it into emptiness–foster development of this awareness.

Practicing at the level of the Hinayana is compared to attempting to retrieve a gem from a muddy pond by standing on the bank with a cup and emptying the dirty water scoop by scoop. Eventually the job gets done, but it's slow going. The Vajrayana is likened to plunging directly into the muck to claim the gem. With indestructible diamond-like Vajrayana awareness, all of life's twists and turns become invitations to compassionately open.

Tibetan Buddhism's Vajrayana teachings and practices, also called *Tantrayana*, are said to be rapid ... but dangerous. Without the foundation of Hinayana discipline and Mahayana compassion, one can be seduced by pleasure, or power, or indulgently rationalize actions driven by self-protective instinctive impulses like anger, fear, and desire. When life is difficult, one can be overwhelmed by the intensity of emotions, deluded by thoughts. Viewing all appearance as fundamentally unreal, one can become mired in a nihilistic, nothing-is-real-therefore-nothing-matters trance.

Learning about these dangers did not dent my commitment; I was undeterred. I didn't want to empty the water in my pond cup by cup. I resolved to hold to the discipline of the Hinayana as best I could, to cultivate the compassion of the Mahayana, and to become like the Bodhisattvas who vowed to be the last to go–remaining in service until every sentient being has been freed from cyclic existence. I was determined to find a way to stay committed to the deity visualization practices. I didn't yet understand the implications of choosing to travel this Tibetan Buddhist path, or where it might lead, but I was willing to do whatever was asked of me–to embrace these foreign, sometimes illogical concepts, to adjust my perceptual kaleidoscopic dial, to think like a Tibetan.

Chapter Eight

DO YOU BELIEVE IN MIRACLES?

Living at the monastery provided unique opportunities to sit with and receive teachings from some of the most senior teachers in Kalu Rinpoche's lineage–like Jamgon Kongtrul Rinpoche, one of the four regents of the *Kagyu* lineage. On a cool November afternoon, as the sun poured in the windows and bounced off the bright yellow walls of the shrine room, thirty-three-year-old Jamgon Kongtrul Rinpoche sat cross-legged on the same silk-covered high seat throne taken by Kalu Rinpoche just a year earlier. Leaning forward, he placed one elbow on the high bench in front of the throne. The residents and a handful of visitors were gathered in the shrine room to hear him. He was speaking–in English–about the importance of maintaining discipline, of following the teachings. He looked completely at home on this seat reserved for teachers of his caliber.

Similar to denominations in the Christian tradition, Tibetan Buddhism has four major lineages: *Kagyu*, *Sakya*, *Nyingma*, and *Gelug*. The Dalai Lama, as the head of the Gelug lineage, traditionally leads the government. Kalu Rinpoche's lineage, the Kagyu, is headed by the *Karmapa*. The Karmapa has four regents, or "heart-sons." And I was receiving teachings from one of them.

The Dalai Lama, the Karmapa, and each of the Karmapa's heart-sons are *tulkus*, reincarnations of spiritual adepts. Honoring their bodhisattva vow, these tulkus have chosen to be reborn again and again, to remain in service. The tulku tradition first began in the thirteenth century with the recognition of the reincarnated Karmapa. About five hundred tulku lineages are still in existence. The current Karmapa is the seventeenth incarnation. The current Dalai Lama is the sixteenth.

Methods for locating these reincarnated teachers developed over many centuries. Traditionally, a group of designated senior lamas look for signs or messages left behind by the deceased teacher regarding the location of his next birth. One of the senior lamas might have a dream revealing details about the house where the reincarnation was born, or of geographical features near the home, or about the parents. Sometimes a rainbow or some other sign in nature appears to guide a search party to the child. Once identified, the child tulku receives a private education from tutors who concentrate on enhancing the child's innate potential for spiritual awakening.

Recognizing a reincarnated master, selecting an heir to a position of power, has fostered controversy, not only during the past centuries, but also more recently. In 1995, the six-year-old Panchen Lama, second to the Dalai Lama in the Gelug lineage, was kidnapped by the Chinese government and replaced with another child. Likely a political prisoner, he's not been seen for decades. The current Dalai Lama, aware that the Chinese government might attempt to interfere in the process of naming his next incarnation, has made it clear that when he returns, his identity will be recognized by his own office—not by China.

Finding the current Karmapa, the seventeenth, has also been problematic. After the sixteenth Karmapa died in Chicago in 1981, the four regent heart-sons couldn't agree on which child was the true reincarnation. This created a rupture in the Kagyu lineage. Currently there are two seventeenth Karmapas.

Several years after his visit to our monastery, heart-son Jamgon Kongtrul Rinpoche was killed in a mysterious car crash. His death was rumored to be connected to the dispute surrounding recognition of the seventeenth Karmapa. But when he graced our small monastery with his visit, I was unaware of the brewing controversy.

From my cushion on the floor in the back of the room, I let my hands rest in my lap and studied the beauty of this heart-son's wide face, his halo of black hair, the joyous ease of his smile. My breath deepened and slowed into waves of contentedness. His presence was so clear, so engaging, that I lost awareness of the content of his words. I was transfixed by the magnificence radiating from his form.

Then, as I continued my heartfelt gaze, his form began to expand. And he continued growing larger until he appeared to be three times his normal size. I blinked rapidly, attempting to clear my vision, scrambling for an explanation. Unlike the menacing giant at the top of Jack's beanstalk grown from magic beans, this giant emanated embracing loving kindness.

After the teaching ended, I joined a couple of nuns in the kitchen to help prepare our dinner. As I chopped potatoes, I waited for someone to mention some kind of unusual occurrence. But no one did.

For the next several months, I attempted to conjure a logical explanation for the appearance of this beneficent giant. I concluded it must have been caused by fatigue. Of course, I hadn't been all that tired. And exhaustion had never caused hallucinations. I decided that maybe I was beginning to think like a Tibetan, to alter my lens. After all, I'd often heard tales of unexplainable phenomena, like stories of yogis in the mountains of Tibet who disappeared with an explosion of rainbow light, leaving behind only their hair and fingernails. During a language lesson, Drupten shared some of translator Yeshe Gyamtso's experiences with Kalu Rinpoche.

"Kalu Rinpoche is pretty frail, right?"

I nodded, "Yes, he's so delicate."

"Well, Yeshe told me that sometimes Rinpoche would grab his hand when they were walking side by side and pull him along. Yeshe said he had to work to keep up with him."

I tilted my head. It didn't seem all that extraordinary. "Sure, but the Tibetans lived in the Himalayas and didn't have the cushy life we have."

He continued, "True. But did you know that for twelve years, beginning when Kalu Rinpoche was about twenty-five, he left the monastery where he grew up and lived in the wilderness of eastern Tibet? Not in a cave either. Just in a niche in the rocks. His nephew would bring him a sack of grain every now and then. Lama Norlha says even the Tibetans wondered how he survived."

I raised my eyebrows in my best "oh, really?" expression.

"Yeah, Yeshe told me that some of the monks who live at Rinpoche's monastery in India said they've seen him fly."

I looked out the window, across the parking lot, toward the barn and my room, wondering if a flying Kalu Rinpoche was a part of an alternative Tibetan Vajrayana reality that could dissolve into emptiness. If so, maybe Jamgon Kongtrul Rinpoche really did grow to three times his normal size. And maybe the disciples actually witnessed Jesus walking on water.

"Do you believe it?" I asked.

Drupten shrugged. "I don't know. Maybe. Why not?"

I nodded, a few more of the bricks jiggling loose in my solid wall of perceived reality. "Why not indeed."

Chapter Nine
RAINBOWS

After months of rising each morning to chant, cleaning houses during the day, returning to chant again, then dinner, more chanting, and finally off to my little room to repeat the Dorje Sempa mantra until I fell asleep, I longed for something, anything, different. And that's what I got.

It was May of 1987. I was sitting on a blanket in a large meadow in Vermont, inhaling pine-scented air and viewing the cremation ceremony of Chögyam Trungpa Rinpoche. This was the same Tibetan master whose photo on Dan's bookshelf had so captivated me back in Oklahoma. My brief stint as a dakini when I first arrived at the monastery was part of the puja performed for his health. Now, once again, he was dancing into my life.

Lama Norlha had organized our travel arrangements. Jodi, a student who recently returned to the monastery, had a reliable Toyota hatchback, so Lama suggested she drive to Vermont with Willa and me as passengers. For the past three years, Jodi had been studying for her nursing degree, then working as a nurse to stockpile the needed funds for the next retreat. Recently, she'd returned to the monastery and moved into the room next to mine, the one previously occupied by Willa. Lama had upgraded Willa's accommodations to one of the larger upstairs rooms.

From the backseat of Jodi's car, I watched Jodi and Willa. Jodi, compact and petite with short brownish-blonde hair, navigated the highway with alert birdlike movements. Willa sat erect, hands in her lap, gazing at the scenery with her tranquil blue eyes. I noted the tight bun on top of her head impeccably holding her wavy, shoulder-length hair.

Maybe Lama's right. I could try to be more like Willa. She really is the ideal student. But I don't see how I can ever manage to be as quietly poised as she is.

No one spoke. Making friends–in fact, participating in any activity deemed a distraction from our practices–was discouraged. Lama had scolded me for my interest in Fourth of July fireworks. "In Tibet, best students never needing, never wanting entertainment. This best, you too. Only practice."

When we first arrived at Chögyam Trungpa Rinpoche's center in Vermont, Jodi pulled up to the entrance gate secured by the Vajra Guards, Western students dressed in khaki uniforms and olive-green berets. She turned to Willa, her eyes darting with an impish grin, "I'll get us in."

She rolled her window down as a Vajra Guard stepped up the car to direct us. "You'll need to find a spot in a lot down the road. Then you can catch one of the buses to ferry back up here. The line to enter the shrine room where the monks are chanting with Trungpa Rinpoche's body starts over there." He pointed to a queue of at least a hundred people. "I can give you a map of the parking areas."

Jodi had other plans. "We're from Kalu Rinpoche's monastery in New York. We're delivering the musical instruments for the ceremonies. Where do we need to take them?"

The back compartment of Jodi's hatchback contained the horns and cymbals we used during our daily pujas. Since Kalu Rinpoche, unlike Chögyam Trungpa Rinpoche, was a traditionalist, our monastery had many of the time-honored instruments used in ceremony. We'd brought the deep, droning bass rag-dung horns which telescope out to eight feet, the oboe-like gyalings, as well as the two types of large brass cymbals. These objects served as our instant entrance pass. The Vajra Guard waved us into the almost-empty parking lot adjoining the center's buildings.

For the past two months, Chögyam Trungpa Rinpoche's students had consulted with Tibetan elders about the elements of traditional cremation rites appropriate for a teacher of Trungpa Rinpoche's status. They learned how to pack their teacher's body in salt according to ancient custom, arranging it inside a wooden box in a meditative seated position. And they constructed a two-story high structure, a *stupa*, for the cremation, using the precise dimensions of those erected for centuries in Tibet.

Chögyam Trungpa Rinpoche was a prominent tulku in the Kagyu lineage. And since he was not only a holder of teachings in the Kagyu tradition, but also those of the Nyingma lineage, senior lamas of both the Kagyu and Nyingma lineages were here in Vermont to assist in performing the cremation ceremonies.

Born in Tibet in 1940, as a young child Chögyam Trungpa Rinpoche was recognized as the eleventh Trungpa reincarnation. He grew up in a monastery, training in meditation and philosophy with senior teachers. At age eight he received ordination as a monk; by eighteen, he completed his studies, obtaining both *Kyorpon* (Doctor of Divinity) and *Khenpo* (Master of Studies) degrees. When he was twenty, with China's invasion of Tibet, he fled his homeland, leading a large group on a perilous nine-month trek across the Himalayas into India.

Just four years after arriving in India, he received a scholarship to study comparative religion at Oxford in England. In this new culture, against the advice of his teachers and without the support of the lineage, he began to explore the possibility of adapting the traditional teachings using Western cultural references and language. Shortly after turning thirty, he blacked out behind the wheel of his car and crashed into a joke shop. The injuries left him partially paralyzed on the left side of his body for the rest of his life. He characterized that event as a "smaller warning," a message that continuing to wear robes and teach in a traditional way created an unnecessary illusion of separation.

After that he really stepped outside the bounds of his tradition. Renouncing his monk's vows, he began working as a lay teacher. The next year he married one of his students (a wealthy English sixteen-year-old named Diana), moved to Vermont, and founded the meditation and retreat center where his body was now being cremated. He established more than one hundred meditation centers throughout the world as well as the Naropa Institute in Boulder, Colorado. Before his death, many of the highest-ranking Tibetan teachers had recognized him as a *Mahasiddha*, a fully enlightened bodhisattva.

I first learned the full extent of Chögyam Trungpa Rinpoche's outside-the-lines behaviors from Drupten. While discussing the possibility of attending the cremation ceremony, Drupten leaned toward me as if sharing an insider's secret. "You know, they called him a crazy wisdom guru."

I'd heard this description of Chögyam Trungpa Rinpoche, but assumed he earned this moniker because he abandoned his monastic vows and modified many of the traditional methods and practices. I looked at Drupten quizzically, "Yes, and...?"

"Well, he smoked and drank. A lot. Even when he was giving teachings. His students never knew for sure when he'd show up; sometimes he kept them waiting for hours. I heard he died of cardiac arrest caused by chronic liver disease. He was only forty-eight years old."

I nodded. None of this was new information.

Drupten continued, "Apparently, he preferred alcohol over taking medication for the pain from his car accident. All that drinking couldn't have been good for his liver."

Drupten looked around the room before continuing. "Did you know he was having sex with his students? He didn't even try to hide it."

I stared at the pecha we were studying, not wanting to continue a conversation about sex with a monk.

"No. No, I haven't heard that." Then I pointed to the page we'd been studying and said, "Hey, let's get started."

After the lesson, as I crossed the parking lot on my way to my room, I attempted to make sense of Drupten's revelations. *Are the norms regarding sex different in Tibetan culture? I know Trungpa Rinpoche wasn't a monk anymore, but what about his marriage vows?*

I'd been able to reason my way into understanding Chögyam Trungpa Rinpoche's choice to drink, but couldn't stretch my sensibilities to accept his having sex with his students, even if he was a crazy wisdom guru. I was grateful to know that Kalu Rinpoche and Lama Norlha would never breach that kind of a boundary.

Shortly after we'd arrived in Vermont, after we dropped off the musical instruments, someone who looked exactly like one of the nuns who was participating in the three-year retreat back in New York waved at me from across the parking lot. This was impossible. No one ever, for any reason, left three-year retreat. Once the retreat began, that was it–the doors were sealed. Other than once-a-week letters going in and out, or Lama visiting to give teachings, the retreatants didn't interface with the world beyond the stockade fence surrounding the retreat building.

Just a month prior to our trip, I found a pair of this nun's sewing scissors in a dining room cabinet I was cleaning out and was advised to send them to her in the retreat house via the weekly mail delivery. So, I packed the scissors in a small box, along with a note asking if she needed anything else. When she didn't respond, I assumed her focus was solely on meditation and practice. But here she was, in Vermont, walking toward me and smiling broadly.

I could only smile back, my awkward silence masking the question I wasn't asking–*Why aren't you in retreat?*

Now standing directly in front of me, she tugged on her zen, straightening it over one shoulder as she answered my unasked question. "A few months ago, I decided retreat just wasn't right for me. I wanted to come back here to be with Trungpa Rinpoche."

I nodded, remembering she'd lived here in Vermont before moving to our monastery to take part in the three-year retreat. "Oh yeah, of course."

Her departure had been a secret. Never mentioned. I assumed she must be embarrassed about leaving the retreat, about her failure, although there were no detectable signs. Smiling again, I could only muster, "So great to see you."

We continued nodding and smiling at each other for a few more moments before she walked away. Once she disappeared into the building, I remembered I hadn't asked if she ever received her sewing scissors. Standing in the parking lot, wondering if I should try to find her, I noticed Jodi walking toward me and called to her. "Hey, do you know what we're supposed to do now? Do we need to do our practices?"

She smiled, "Well, we could check out the chanting the lamas are doing with Chögyam Trungpa Rinpoche's body in the shrine room. Drupten and Dechi are in there."

I was delighted that she seemed as ambivalent as I was about accumulating mantras while on our fully sanctioned road trip.

When we entered the main building, about thirty of Chögyam Trungpa Rinpoche's students were beginning to file into the shrine room. We casually slipped into the line. Once inside we found a spot on the floor in the small area designated for the groups of viewers.

Clouds of incense and the drone of chanting filled the air. I craned my neck, wriggling in an attempt to view the box holding Trungpa Rinpoche's body. But it was hidden behind a column. Dechi and Drupten were seated with the rows of Tibetan monks, their eyes glued to the chanting pechas. I tried not to stare at Dilgo Khyentse Rinpoche, head of the Nyingma lineage, who was leading the chanting. He was the largest Tibetan I'd ever seen, a non-bearded Santa with receding slicked-back white hair and naked above the waist.

After fifteen minutes, our group was ushered out to make room for the next. But instead of dutifully leaving the area like the rest of the students, Jodi and I sauntered back into the line, joining the next group as they entered. We viewed the chanting once again, then filed out and for a third time found a place in the line of students waiting to enter.

Just then Pema Chödrön, a Western nun and director of Gampo Abbey, Trungpa Rinpoche's monastery in Nova Scotia, pulled us aside. Quietly she pleaded, "You're taking spots in the room meant for Rinpoche's students. They've traveled here from around the world for the last chance to spend a few minutes with their teacher's body."

I stared at the ground. This was not the behavior of a bodhisattva, not putting myself last. With this reminder, we immediately left the area and returned to our room, where we found Willa seated on the floor, eyes closed, mala in hand.

The next morning in the pre-dawn light, Willa, Jodi, and I quietly walked up to the meadow, the site of the cremation ceremony. It was overcast and foggy, a light mist falling. I wondered if the rain might interfere with the cremation fire, but as the sun rose and more and more attendees silently filled the meadow, the sky cleared.

In the quiet, pristine expanse of the now vibrantly blue sky, three birds with massive wingspans appeared, soaring in circles directly above the ornate cremation stupa. Chögyam Trungpa Rinpoche's body would soon be placed inside this twenty-five-foot-high vase-like structure with a golden spire. The gliding birds brushed a silent stillness across the meadow, circling in larger and larger loops until they disappeared.

After the sun fully cleared the horizon, the sound of a single bagpiper and the slow, steady heartbeat of a deep bass drum signaled the approach of the funeral procession. The guttural wailing of Tibetan horns–the instruments we'd transported–pierced the still air. I spotted Dechi and Drupten in the single-file line preceding the body. They each held a tall wooden pole supporting one of four huge banners–red, white, yellow, and green. Dechi carried the sunflower yellow, Drupten the forest green.

Next came the Vajra Guards, in khaki uniforms, carrying the palanquin–the canopied, silk-curtained wooden box containing Rinpoche's body. When they reached the stupa, the guards climbed several wooden stairs and lifted the box into the middle section of the structure. The Kagyu teachers and monks began to chant on one side of the stupa, the Nyingma teachers and monks on another. On the third side, a large group of Trungpa Rinpoche's most advanced students chanted an English translation of a traditional Tibetan puja ritual.

For the next three hours, as the chanting continued, the more than two thousand observers lined up in silent queue. One by one, we each offered a *kata*–a long thin white silk scarf–placing it on one of the piles at the base of the stupa. Finally, after we all filed past and returned to our places in the surrounding meadow, a cannon was fired, and the fire was lit. Bagpipes droned. A ringing mixture of Tibetan horns, drums, bells, and cymbals pierced the midday air.

As smoke began to rise from the stupa, a group of Tibetans, dressed in Western clothing and sitting near us in the meadow, began pointing. Long thin wisps of clouds shaped like horse tails were wafting through the sky that had earlier been so vibrantly clear.

Willa walked over to the Tibetans who seemed insistent we recognize something about the wavy clouds. She returned smiling, "They said those are kata clouds. The local deities are pleased. They told me this is what happens in Tibet when a high lama is cremated." Surveying the thin clouds, I noted that they were indeed shaped like the kata scarves we'd offered at the cremation stupa.

Waves of chanting continued floating through the meadow as flakes of ash drifted in the wind. Those kata clouds were just the pre-show. Gradually, another much larger elongated rainbow cloud began to fill the sky. Undulating with streaks of turquoise, rose, and purple, fingers of color fanned out in a dragon-like shape, as if a huge watercolor brush was sweeping waves of light across the sky–blues and pinks topped with feathery plumes of yellows and oranges. The colors appeared even more vivid through my polarized sunglasses. Many of the observers in the meadow began pointing, murmuring, and then gently applauding.

As I continued watching, mesmerized by the transparent multi-colored manifestation, a gentle penetrating pressure began to pull at the area behind my breastbone, as if my chest was being lovingly stretched open by the hands of an invisible surgeon. I was engulfed in a timeless sense of peace and acceptance. Even though I'd never met Chögyam Trungpa Rinpoche, I was certain he was the essence of this dancing rainbow.

After the cremation ceremony ended, as the sun began to drift toward the western horizon, we silently hiked back toward Jodi's car for the drive home. Walking past the long lines of students waiting for the buses to shuttle them back to the distant lots, I reflected on the sights and sounds–the clouds, the rainbows, the intense experience of openness and peace–struggling to concoct a logical explanation.

Those thin clouds were unusual, yes ... but I've seen clouds kind of like that before. Maybe they were a meteorological coincidence.

But what about that rainbow display? Could it have been caused by heat from the cremation fire? I've never seen a rainbow anything like that. And it certainly wasn't my imagination—everyone saw it.

I watched my footfalls creating barely visible prints in the dirt. Unable to find any easy logic for the penetrating heart opening, for the expansive, yet silent, loving stillness, for my sense of having been in Chögyam Trungpa Rinpoche's presence, I told myself it must have been a result of being surrounded by all those devoted students. Then, I glanced up at the western sky. A rainbow halo completely encircled the late afternoon sun.

Chapter Ten

PALDEN DROLMA

On the seventh of January, 1988, I was in Bodh Gaya, India, pacing around a monastery courtyard. The moon shone bright orange through the polluted, dusty skies on this mild night. Looking up at the dark window of Kalu Rinpoche's room, I had serious doubts about my intention to become a Tibetan Buddhist nun the next day.

Bodh Gaya is where the Buddha is said to have attained enlightenment while sitting under the sprawling, still-present Bodhi tree. We'd been assured taking vows here was a guarantee of also attaining enlightenment–in this lifetime. While I hoped this was true, I assumed this was akin to making a wish before blowing out my birthday candles, and I'd long ago abandoned any real confidence in birthday wishes coming true.

Prior to the trip, after Lama shared Willa's plans to take vows of ordination to become a nun in India, I concluded I should too. It didn't seem like a big leap at the time–Roberta became Trinley when she received these vows before starting her three-year retreat. This was just another natural step on the road to retreat and transcendence. Learning that Jodi also intended to take vows in India deepened my resolve. After all, taking vows was a way to become a member of the team. And this team promised enlightenment.

But what if I'd been wrong? Leaping into the life of a renunciate, embracing this Technicolor, deity-filled faith from another part of the world was beginning to feel like folly.

Lama had first planned this trip to India so we could experience the grace of being in Kalu Rinpoche's presence. Because of his aging body, it was unlikely Rinpoche would be able to return to the States, but he could travel from his home monastery in Sonada to Bodh Gaya. While here, he was offering ritual initiation empowerment ceremonies for many of the Vajrayana practices–including those taught in retreat. A practice isn't considered fully effective until its fundamental essence, its power, has been transmitted by a qualified teacher. To receive these ceremonial transmissions from a master of Kalu Rinpoche's caliber was auspicious–and rare. Even though a few of us (including me) had already received the empowerments for the retreat practices, repetition promised additional blessing.

Shortly after arriving in Bodh Gaya, we were shown to our living quarters. The women were given a large, empty, upstairs room with a row of high windows opposite the door. We purchased cotton-filled, two-inch-thick mats covered in beige muslin from the town market and placed them with our sleeping bags onto the concrete floor. I claimed a spot in the farthest corner from the door, the most private location I could find.

Many nights, jarring Bollywood-style music broadcast from neighborhood loudspeakers filtered through the windows. But this night was quiet. No music, just moonlight. In contrast to the noise of my doubting thoughts, the room was silent, other than some sleep breathing. With my spiraling apprehension in full swing, I'd tiptoed across the dark room, gingerly opened the door, slipped out, and padded down the stairs to the courtyard.

Pacing on the concrete, I glanced again and again toward Kalu Rinpoche's window. I hadn't received a list of the thirty-six vows we'd be taking the next day. But the tightness in my chest and belly and my shallow breath weren't a result of this lack of information. I knew we'd promise to not kill, not steal, not lie (especially to not lie about spiritual attainment), not become intoxicated (no drugs or alcohol), not have sex (particularly no orgasm), not let our hair grow longer than the width of two fingers, not wear ordinary clothes (we must dress in the robes of an ordained person), and not eat after the noon meal.

I imagined that once we arrived in India, prior to the vow-taking ceremony, we'd receive special instruction on each of the thirty-six vows. But that hadn't happened. Months earlier, shortly after I announced my intention to take vows in India, Drupten paused during one of our language lessons, his face surprisingly stern, "You know you're going to vow to never cover your rice with the vegetables." Then he laughed. "Not only that, you also won't be able to cover your vegetables with the rice." That was the last I heard about those two vows, so I reasoned any unrevealed vows of the thirty-six were either outdated or not necessary in our wealthy Western culture.

I also wasn't concerned about forgoing eating after lunch. Dinner could include anything classified as a liquid–like soups full of chunks of beef or a bowl of yogurt loaded with jam or sugar. I clearly wasn't promising to go hungry in the evening for the rest of my life. Surprisingly, I wasn't particularly anxious about getting rid of my hair, nor even with never having sex again. In fact, I hoped taking vows would finally end my lingering fantasies of rekindling an intimate relationship with Dan. I was moving on. In my fantasy future encounter with Dan, I, wearing robes and lacking hair, would smile reverently, assured and peaceful.

And I was no longer troubled by the misogynous elements of the Tibetan culture and religion I'd encountered after arriving in India. A week earlier, this worry flared when Dechi announced her prayer to be reborn as a man in her next lifetime–so she'd be able to attain enlightenment. The benefit of incarnating in a male body was mentioned in our regularly chanted Tibetan liturgies, but until Dechi's pronouncement I'd concluded this notion was simply another remnant of outdated theology–like the prohibition of hiding vegetables or rice.

But here, camped out in the heart of Buddha-land, in this Tibetan monastery, I noted the seating arrangement in the shrine room and the order of the queue to receive blessings, meals, or tea. Monks first, nuns last. I'd heard that in traditional Tibetan culture, the hierarchy of class was monks, men, women–and lastly, nuns. Nuns were at the bottom of the food chain.

I began to wonder if Dechi was privy to a greater depth of teachings. How could a nun who'd completed three-year retreat believe this concept? What if, as a nun in this religion, I didn't have a shot at enlightenment? How did that square with Bodh Gaya's assurance of enlightenment-in-this-lifetime? Even if this promise was simply a wishful caveat, was it only applicable to men?

The vows Willa, Jodi, and I planned to receive were for novice-level ordination. Yet, all the monks at our monastery in New York were able to receive full ordination–*Gelong* vows. But the nun's version of the Gelong vows, the Tibetan *Gelongma* lineage, had been lost eight hundred years earlier when a group of the eleven nuns required to administer the rites could no longer be found. A monk's full Gelong ordination requires over two hundred and fifty vows. However, based on early Buddhist teachings on the inferiority of women, Gelongma ordination, when it was available, required over a hundred more.

After Dechi's proclamation and my ensuing doubt storm regarding misogyny, I approached Lama Norlha to inquire why I'd want to join a discriminatory system. He looked at me with an odd mixture of concern and annoyance, "Not like this in America, at home. Nuns-monks, same-same."

It was true. The nuns in our center not only had positions of authority equal to the monks, but Lama's head administrator was a nun. The nuns had built the center alongside the monks and received the same teachings, the same opportunities. One of Lama's favorite students, certainly his favorite female student, was Tsupa, star of the last retreat. Tall, angular, finely-boned and stern, she was clearly as strong as any of the monks. She was designated student leader and Lama's translator in the women's retreat in which Trinley was participating. More than once I'd heard Lama praise the nuns in retreat. He'd even declared their steady, disciplined focus to be superior to that of the monks. As far as I could discern, nuns truly weren't second-class citizens at our monastery.

So, it wasn't an apprehension about misogyny that had pulled me out of bed. Not a lack of information, not a concern about no longer having dinner, or hair, or sex. The source of my distress was closer to the bone.

Earlier that day I'd met with Kalu Rinpoche one on one. In that first private meeting with Rinpoche, one of the two in my lifetime, Lama Norlha served as translator. I was sure speaking directly with this enlightened master would result in an experience, a connection, or at the very least, a hint of certainty that I belonged.

First, I requested permission to take vows. Kalu Rinpoche nodded yes.

I continued, "If I become a nun, will I have a good outcome?"

Kalu Rinpoche indicated his yes with the gentlest smile.

Next, I asked permission to forgo wearing robes, to dress in street clothes while working my cleaning jobs. Again, Kalu Rinpoche bobbed his head in the affirmative.

Finally, I asked a question about the nature of reality. With much deliberation I'd crafted this question just the day before. After all, this was my chance to get a scoop on the big secret. I read the penciled words of my question from the index card I was holding.

"When I look to find myself in my body, I can't find anything. Nothing is there. But an awareness is always doing the looking. It's not something I can see or touch, but I know it exists in the same way I know an atom exists, even though I've never seen one. So how can emptiness and existence both be true?"

After I read my question, Lama Norlha translated. Kalu Rinpoche looked directly at me, gently smiling and nodding, just like he had when answering my protocol questions about taking vows and clothing.

I took a breath. That was it. That was the answer.

I looked at Kalu Rinpoche and then at Lama.

Lama smiled as he waved his hand motioning for me to leave, "Good, you go now."

The meeting was over. I'd finally had a chance to meet with Kalu Rinpoche and nothing had changed. I left the room and paused in the damp silence of the stone stairway. *Maybe Rinpoche thinks I'm not developed enough, not capable of understanding his response.*

It would be years before I'd come to appreciate the depth of truth in Kalu Rinpoche's nodded yes, his confirmation of the apparent contradiction. My question was a koan, unanswerable with the logical mind.

But now, pacing in the courtyard, I was only cognizant of that familiar, empty, you're-on-your-own-here feeling. *Maybe I'll never measure up. Maybe I just don't belong here, don't fit.* This roaring apprehension could not be reasoned away. *What if taking nun's vows is just another attempt to get Lama's approval–another way to try to keep up with Willa?*

My mind racing, I again gazed at Kalu Rinpoche's window, then at the moon and the stars. As I paced back and forth in the courtyard, hoping, praying for an answer or a sign, the steady, methodical heartbeat of a Tibetan drum penetrated the night air.

The drumbeat came from the one-story building on my right

where Lama Norlha was staying. The rhythmic sound of the drum was joined by a ringing Tibetan bell, then a wailing eerie ah-oo from a thighbone trumpet horn, a *kangling*. Lama Norlha was performing *Chod* practice. Chod translates as "cutting through," clearing away the obscurations of the human mind. My swirling doubt and sense of not belonging were perfect manifestations of a fully obscured mind.

The Chod drumbeat is produced by holding a two-sided, twelve-inch cylindrical drum and flipping the wrist to twirl the drum back and forth, back and forth. This motion causes two spheres of weighted fabric to alternately hit the green drumskins. The kangling is played much like a trumpet, but from the side of the mouth. It's about twelve inches long, made from a hollowed out human femur. Its sound is a compassionate call to suffering demons, an offering up of oneself to those forces, a full-hearted surrender.

The Chod drumbeat cut through the thick, still air. Beat-beat ... beat-beat ... beat-beat. The steady rumble of the drum, followed by the high-pitched metallic ring of the bell, then the cry of the kangling, permeated the night air, permeated me. I stopped pacing. I knew Lama Norlha was chanting, ringing his bell, then putting it down to pick up the kangling and place it to his lips, all the while maintaining a constant drumbeat with the wooden drum in his right hand.

Without intention or effort, as if my fairy godmother had appeared and waved her calming magic wand, the swell of intense doubt began to quiet, then disappear. When the Chod practice ended, only thick silence remained. And clarity.

I'm in India. I've come all this way to become a nun. That's what I'm going to do.

But I had a condition.

Part of the taking vows ceremony is receiving a new name. I wanted a good one. Looking again directly at Kalu Rinpoche's window, I dared to wish for a name like Tara. Arya Tara, the green-skinned goddess of compassion, the mother of the Buddhas, the deity whose twenty-one praises we chanted at least seven times each morning–the same twenty-one praises Lama Norlha had repeated one million times prior to walking out of the Chinese prison camp on the night of a full moon, unseen by the tower guards.

I didn't want an ordinary name. I knew names were sometimes given to designate qualities a student possessed, like Yeshe Gyamtso's, Ocean of Wisdom. But sometimes the name represents qualities needing enhancement. I didn't want a name like Tsupa (Tsultrim Palmo), Woman of Discipline, even though she was one of Lama's favorite nuns. Or Gendun Chopel, Helper Who Spreads the Dharma. Or Sonam Wangmo, Powerful Merit. Or Dechi Palmo, Woman of Bliss and Happiness. Or Trinley Wangmo, Powerful Activity. If I was going to become a nun, I wanted a big name, an important name.

In the fresh, still silence, I glanced up at Kalu Rinpoche's window one more time, then climbed the stairs and slipped back into our room. Snuggling into my sleeping bag, I smiled at the audacity of my request, certain it would soon fade, like all of my birthday wishes.

The next afternoon, after a shower in the concrete cold-water shower room, after Willa, Jodi and I had our heads shaved for the first time by Lama Norlha with his golden double-edged blade razor, after rinsing our only slightly nicked heads with a green water hose, after donning our yellow cotton shirts and *tonga* vests, after Dechi expertly helped us fold the skirt-making tube of yards of fabric around our bodies, after learning how to properly wrap and hold our shawl-like zens, we joined about twenty squirmy eight and nine-year-old Tibetan boys in the shrine room of the monastery to receive novice vows. As instructed, we each had collected several strips of yellow cloth to be used in the ceremony. These pieces of fabric would become the representation of our vows, like rings in a marriage ceremony. Later we'd sew the strips of cloth into a little packet to wear next to our bodies for the rest of our lives.

I have little memory of the exact elements of the vow-taking ceremony. But as in every other transmission ritual, we approached Kalu Rinpoche on his high throne seat multiple times– to receive blessings, to touch a sacred object, to be sprinkled with water, to be bopped on the head by peacock feathers. When Lama Norlha shaved our heads, he left a small tassel of hair on the rear crown. One pass of the ceremony involved snipping it off. Finally, Kalu Rinpoche handed each of us an envelope containing a piece of his official stationery on which he'd written our new names. We weren't to open our envelopes until after the ceremony.

When we exited the shrine room, Lama Norlha was waiting for us in the courtyard. We gathered around him, each pulling the piece of ivory stationery out of its envelope. I stared at Kalu Rinpoche's shaky writing. I could read Tibetan print, but my new name was written in Tibetan cursive, beyond my grasp.

Lama read Jodi's slip of paper first.

"Chodrin Palmo. You be Chodrin. Lamp of Dharma."

Next, he read Willa's.

"Tsultrim Palmo. We call you Palmo."

Kalu Rinpoche had given Willa the same name as Lama Norlha's star student, Tsupa, Tsultrim Palmo. Instead of making a contraction of the full name as he had for Tsupa, Lama decided Willa would be called simply Palmo.

Then he read mine.

"Palden Drolma. Paldrom."

Palden Drolma in Tibetan translates as Glorious Female One Who Liberates. In Sanskrit, she is Arya Tara, Glorious Tara.

I stared at a building across the courtyard. The fact of this name was so unexpected, so unbelievable, my mind stopped. This was not a meditative stillness, but a stun. *How could I have dared to even imagine asking for such a thing?*

Jodi, newly Chodrin, cocked her head. "Do you remember when we went up for our names? We lined up in a different order than we had for the other blessings."

I didn't remember that.

She continued, "Yeah, Rinpoche noticed and rearranged the order of the envelopes. He chose special names for each of us."

Our names had not been randomly assigned. Kalu Rinpoche had indeed specifically named me Palden Drolma.

That evening, just as we had each day since arriving in Bodh Gaya, we gathered in the open tent structure behind the monastery for our dinner of *dahl* and white rice. Lama Norlha cooked the lentil and curry dahl in a massive pot that rested on a gas burner placed outside our dining tent. The mushy concoction always had a slightly charred quality. After a few more weeks I'd no longer be able to stomach the smoky curried lentils, so resorted to eating only white rice seasoned with ketchup I purchased from a stand in the market.

But on that first night as a nun, no thoughts of liking or disliking arose. The next day Lama Norlha would instruct us, the newly ordained, to abstain from eating all foods (including those classified as liquids) after lunch for the next thirty days. This would demonstrate respect for our new vows. The temporary, full compliance with this one particular vow wasn't a problem. Questioning and doubt would return, but for now were on holiday.

After everyone left the dining tent, as the air chilled and the sun began to set, I wrapped myself in the warmth of the yards of fabric of my new burgundy wool zen shawl. I watched the oversized orange Indian sun disappear, its vanishing light filtering through the smoke-filled, charcoal-scented air of Bodh Gaya. It was quiet. I was quiet.

In the silence of that moment, embraced by the robes of this lineage of monks, nuns, saints, and sages, I felt a relaxation, a lack of seeking. How many, many ways had I struggled to be a part of a family, to belong?

I was now Paldrom, Tara, mother of the Buddhas. I'd prayed to be a Tara, a deity, not recognizing I was also asking to be named for The Mother. In time I've come to realize the perfection, the gift, the blessing, of this name. I was named for the quality I was most deeply seeking, the seed of my desire to be enlightened–the source of mothering, of belonging, of acceptance, of home.

Chapter Eleven
CELIBACY

The flap of the rickshaw's skinny tires on the dirt road and the high-pitched woot-toot of its horn mingled with the cool night air whipping across my almost-bald scalp. Lama Norlha and I were sharing this rickshaw ride. Each time the driver swerved to avoid a sacred cow in the middle of the road, I pushed my feet against the floorboard and pressed my right hip into the cold metal railing to remain as erect as I could on the hard seat. I certainly didn't want to topple over onto Lama.

Protected from the nippy air, cozy in my yards of burgundy wool, I rubbed my palm across the top of my head, enjoying the downy softness of my quarter-inch halo of hair. It had been only a few days since we'd left Bodh Gaya's monastery, where one of the perks of having a shaved head was shorter cold-water showers–I could wash my stubble with a wet wipe. But now we were staying at a real motel with hot water, a bathtub and shower, a flush toilet, beds, pristine angelically white sheets and towels, even room service. I was assigned to share a room with the newly-named Palmo (formerly Willa).

We'd stopped in the Darjeeling region at the base of the Himalayan foothills before traveling on to Kalu Rinpoche's home monastery in Sonada. Lama intended our three-day stay to be "a rest and vacation for Kalu Rinpoche." Shortly after we arrived, he arranged a scenic lake boat ride for Rinpoche. And we got to tag along–Lama's ducklings.

As we filed onto the boat trailing Lama and Rinpoche, I recalled something Chodrin (no longer Jodi) mentioned earlier in the day. In Bodh Gaya, she overheard two Western women who'd also traveled to see Kalu Rinpoche. They were commenting about us, Lama's three newest nuns. Jodi pursed her lips, "They called us the Norlettes." The look on her face indicated she knew this wasn't meant as a compliment.

Lama Norlha and Kalu Rinpoche sauntered to the front of the boat as it purred along in the water. Immediately a few birds landed in front of them on the boat's edge. This seemed a special delight for Lama and Rinpoche. As they continued watching the wild birds, Lama urged Kalu Rinpoche, via demonstration, to hold his arms straight out, like a scarecrow. With a brief grin, Rinpoche positioned his arms as Lama directed. Within thirty seconds, two birds landed on each of Rinpoche's arms, then two more, and two more, until his arms filled with birds. No one said a word. We just glanced at each other, then back at Kalu Rinpoche. I took a deep breath of the moist air and smiled. *I'm lucky, even blessed to be here. Being a Norlette has some pretty great perks.*

That evening, back in the cushy motel room, sitting on my bed, I pulled my legs up against my chest. *Maybe those birds were attracted to Rinpoche because he lived for so many years in that niche in the rocks. Even wild birds feel something safe and welcoming. Hey, if I were a bird, I'd want to land on his arms too.*

Palmo and I had ordered tea from room service to accompany our individual practices. I poured the steamy, golden brown Darjeeling tea from the ivory ceramic teapot into our thick mugs. We didn't chat. We had Dorje Sempa mantras to recite. Palmo put the teacup to her lips and blew on the surface of the tea, but it was still too hot to drink.

She placed the cup on the bedside table, sat cross-legged on her bed, closed her eyes, and began repeating the mantra.

I added cream and sugar to my cup, making the tea just cool enough to sip. It was the most delicious tea I'd ever tasted, as if contentment had been steeped into the cup. Maybe it was because the tea had been freshly picked–it was locally grown Darjeeling tea. Or maybe it was the comfort of being in a clean motel room away from the grimy, polluted air of Bodh Gaya. Maybe I was still basking in receiving vows, wearing robes, now feeling a part of this Tibetan Buddhist family. Or maybe it was being just a few rooms away from Kalu Rinpoche. Whatever the reason, in that moment my concern with being more like Palmo, with winning my covert Dorje Sempa mantra repetition competition, dissolved into emptiness like the deities at the end of a practice. Taking another sip of the nectar-like tea, remembering Kalu Rinpoche and the birds, I breathed in the fullness of belonging.

A knock at our door pulled me from my reverie. Palmo didn't open her eyes, so I hopped off the white bedspread to see who it was. I was surprised to see Lama when I opened the door.

He smiled broadly. "Paldrom, come help. Need butter for Rinpoche's tea. We go to bazaar to buy." I couldn't imagine why Lama needed my help to buy butter in the market. But as he turned and headed down the hall, I slipped on my flip-flops and followed.

Several rickshaw drivers had congregated at the entrance to the hotel and Lama called one over. Even though he was speaking in Hindi, I could discern he was asking the driver to take us to the market, then negotiating a price. Lama climbed onto the rickshaw seat, and with a flick of his head, indicated I should join him.

The driver took off, pedaling with such vigor I concluded Lama must have negotiated a speedy trip. Once we arrived at the marketplace, Lama jumped out and glanced back over his shoulder, "Wait here."

I detected a slight whiff of cow dung and pulled my zen across my face. *Maybe Lama just needed someone to ride along so the rickshaw driver would wait for him at the market. Still, he picked me. Me, not Palmo.... Oh geez. What am I thinking? Why do I care so much? What's wrong with me? I wish I could stop comparing myself to her. But Lama encouraged me to pay attention to her greatness, to try to be more like her.*

Returning within minutes, Lama handed me a blue opaque plastic bag with two blocks of cold butter, smiling for just a moment. Grabbing onto the metal rail of the rickshaw, he hopped onto the seat beside me. Without a word, the driver began enthusiastically pedaling back toward the hotel.

Sitting next to Lama, our hips just barely touching on the cracked leather seat, the rickshaw jolting noisily along the bumpy road, and the cool wind pressing against my cheeks, I felt a surge of sexual desire. It had been months since any thought of sex had entered my mind. Preparing to come to India, traveling, taking vows–just being here–had been all-consuming.

I straightened my shoulders and took a deep breath. *Whoa. How inappropriate. I'm a nun. I took a vow of celibacy. This is my Lama. Now I'm really going off the deep end. Could Lama know what I just felt?*

Without turning my head, I peeked at Lama. In the glow of the string of lights along the roadside, his face was expressionless.

That night, as I lay under the crisp white sheets, Palmo quietly asleep in the twin bed next to me, I watched the moonlight streaming through the window, wondering about that sexual rush. *Where did it come from? Is this going to become a problem for me? Does anyone else have this issue? Or wonder about it? Or ever talk about it?*

I recalled how, just two days earlier, Lama had pulled me aside in a hallway at the Delhi hotel where we stopped for the night. He took a step toward me and touched my arm. "Now you are a nun. Anything you need, you say. I take care of you."

I smiled. "Thank you, Lama."

It seemed odd. He'd never talked like that before, never stood that close. I wasn't sure what kind of "anything" he meant.

Now nestled in bed, I imagined Kalu Rinpoche in his room sipping Tibetan-style tea with salt and the butter from the market. I rolled over, curling up on my side. *Could Lama have been offering something sexual in the hallway in Delhi? Was he offering sex as a way to keep me in the fold? Is this what it means to be a Norlette?* I didn't know–and this certainly wasn't the first time I'd struggled to find clarity in this Tibetan world.

When I first learned about the Vajrayana Tantric yab-yum practices–visualizing oneself as both a male and female deity in sexual embrace–I recognized how the practices were using the power of the sexual urge to open the body's channels, first focusing on the warmth of the sexual drive in the groin, the second chakra, then imagining the energy flowing upwards through energetic channels, opening them, clearing them. I understood preserving and using this sexual energy as the purpose of the vow of celibacy. Physical sexual contact impairs the vow, but having an orgasm, releasing the powerful sexual energy, breaks it.

I knew about the transformative power of sexual energy. One late afternoon in Oklahoma, while Dan and I were having sex, he placed one of his hands on the top of my head, the other on my sacrum. The intensity of my desire, combined with the potency of my love, surrender, and devotion, somehow generated an internal, electrical force as undeniable as an Oklahoma windstorm. My entire body shook like a fish pulled from its watery home. Dan told me to just let go and ride the energies. So I did.

After that, my nervous system was never quite the same. I've learned this kind of shaking indicates a blockage, a channel needing to be opened or cleaned out. Still today, when I experience an intense emotion, or when there's a sudden loud noise, my head might give a little involuntary bobblehead shake. My channels still require some dross removal. But this type of lingering effect isn't unusual. Hindu sage Ramana Maharshi explained, "Once an elephant enters the tent, the tent is never the same."

My feelings in the rickshaw with Lama were a clear indication that receiving vows hadn't removed my body's natural desire for sex. After returning to our monastery in New York, I continued to experience fleeting sexual urges, sometimes out of nowhere, like when simply driving home from a cleaning job. It was one thing to push the boundaries of vows by abstaining from eating after the noon meal by "drinking" soup and yogurt for dinner, or eating meat only from large animals, but I was clear about the value of strictly maintaining the vow of celibacy.

Even though I had difficulty learning to speak Tibetan, wasn't a natural meditator, and couldn't seem to control my comparisons (or any of my emotions), I was grateful I knew how to simply feel the warm glow of my sexual urges, to imagine the energy moving up through invisible channels. I surrendered to my vow of celibacy, understanding it to be a support to becoming enlightened.

This surrender didn't eliminate my sexual desire. Some nights, lying on my little cot-sized bed, I dreamt of beginning to have sex with Dan. But even with Dream Dan, I'd stop myself, saying, "I cannot do this. I will not break my vow."

Chapter Twelve

IN KALU RINPOCHE'S ROOM

After several days at the cushy motel, it was time for our next stop–Kalu Rinpoche's home monastery in Sonada, just west of Nepal and south of Tibet. Lama hired several taxis for the hour-long trip and, at his direction, Dechi, Palmo, Chodrin, and I crammed into the back seat of one. At first glance, squeezing all four of us onto the seat looked impossible. But Lama had a plan. We each sat at a slight angle and staggered ourselves–two perched on the front edge of the seat, the other two as far back as possible. Palmo and I sat on the outer edges, our hips shoved into the door handles.

As the driver flew up the mountainous roads, climbing to our destination of 6,700 feet, my lungs filled with the cold, damp, thinning air. Each turn brought widening views of the Himalayas. But even this majesty couldn't alleviate my fear that at any moment the speeding driver would misjudge the angle of a sharp curve and we'd plunge off the mountainside. When we finally pulled up in front of the multi-tiered white monastery building, I loosened my clenched fingers and breathed out my relief.

The sun, peeking through the gray sky, illuminated the monastery's burgundy trim decorated with small wooden blocks, elaborately painted in white, lilac, and moss green. The multicolored intricacy of the building and the alive green of the surrounding hills stood in sharp contrast to the gray, barren pavement stretching like an empty playground in front of the monastery buildings.

Immediately after we arrived, Lama directed us to our living quarters. Our group of nuns was assigned to a windowless little shrine room on the far side of the monastery grounds. After lugging our large suitcases down a winding dirt path, we settled in by opening our luggage and rolling our sleeping bags out onto the cold floor. I wished we'd been able to bring the cotton-filled mats we purchased in Bodh Gaya, but quickly realized they'd never fit into those taxis.

Our only assignment during the five-week stay was to work on our individual practices. We could walk around the grounds, eat at the dining hall, or join the resident monks for their morning and evening pujas. For hours each day, with eyes closed, I passed each of the 108 beads of my mala slowly through my thumb and forefinger, moving one bead after each recitation of the one hundred syllables while visualizing Dorje Sempa resting directly above my head, his big toe pouring his purifying white light into my body, removing negativity.

Keeping track of the rounds of 108 repetitions is accomplished with an abacus system, using two sets of ten miniature brass rings and a tiny brass clip (mine was shaped like a lotus) attached to the mala's beads. I'd threaded my brass rings onto a thin strip of purple grosgrain ribbon. My mala's mocha-colored rosewood beads had darkened to a shiny deep chocolate from being repeatedly rubbed through my fingers. But as many times as I chanted the mantra, as many times as I filled myself with Dorje Sempa's creamy cleansing white light, I couldn't stop competing with Palmo. I was secretly hoping she wouldn't be able to complete the 111,111 repetitions of Dorje Sempa's mantra before I did.

At mealtimes, I covertly eyed the tracking counters hanging on her mala, each day becoming more convinced she was catching up ... and possibly surpassing me. The more I compared myself to her, trying to be like her (as Lama had instructed), the more the tendrils of my deficiency began to weaken and crack the solid peace of belonging I'd felt in the dining tent in Bodh Gaya. Not a sliver of the contentment I'd experienced while sipping tea in the cushy motel room remained. I so wanted the approving smiles Lama sent her way.

One chilly afternoon, two weeks after we arrived, Palmo and I sat on our sleeping bags on the floor of the dark little shrine room, doing our practices. But instead of focusing on Dorje Sempa's purifying white light, I found myself only listening to Palmo's chanting. Lama had advised us to chant softly, just loud enough to hear ourselves, yet as she chanted, I could clearly make out every syllable.

Glaring in her direction, I began to simmer. *Does she know how loud she is? Is she showing off? Oh, why do I care so much? Why can't I just focus on my own practice?*

Every overheard syllable became a reminder of my inferiority, my lack of capacity–a confirmation that I'd never measure up. I silently stormed from the room and took a long walk around the monastery grounds, incapable of practicing for the rest of the day.

That evening, seated on a hill overlooking the lights flickering from Kalu Rinpoche's window, I pictured him peacefully meditating, or chanting–exactly what I was supposed to be doing. But here I was with my shaved head and burgundy robes, feeling sorry for myself, crying in the dark. Joining this family of the Buddha hadn't changed anything after all.

As the wind whipped through the pines, I pulled my zen tightly around my shoulders, trying to stay warm. *I have no idea how to work with my out-of-control mind. I'm hopeless. I've had enough. Please Rinpoche, just let me die.*

Shifting on the dirt, I recalled my silent appeal in the monastery courtyard in Bodh Gaya–and its success. So I reconsidered my request. *Even if getting my name was a fluke, or a coincidence, the*

Tibetans say a master teacher like Kalu Rinpoche is a wish-fulfilling gem. What I really want is a way to stop feeling everything so much—to stop being angry, to stop competing, to stop suffering. I so want to be serene and composed, but I just don't know how.

This was the reason I longed for enlightenment—as a balm for this very suffering. And even though I'd taken vows as a nun, had completed more than 111,111 prostrations, had repeated Dorje Sempa's mantra over fifty thousand times, even though I was trying to become more like Palmo, nothing seemed to work. *I just don't know what to do. Rinpoche, please help me.*

With the clarity of this plea, a bit of relief began warming in my chest. I returned to our little shrine room, slipped into my sleeping bag, and snuggled in its warmth.

The next morning Lama announced that he'd arranged for us to meet with Kalu Rinpoche in his private room. We were to receive special instructions on the practice we chanted each evening after dinner—Chenrezig, the bodhisattva embodying the essence of loving compassion.

That afternoon we silently filed into Kalu Rinpoche's room. Those of us holding vows entered first. The only sound was the thump of our knees, then the quiet tap of hands, then forehead on the floor, followed by the rustle of the yards of fabric as we rose again to standing. Finally, with a quick flip of the zen over one shoulder, we brought our hands together in prayer, touching forehead, mouth, heart. Three times, knees, hands, forehead to floor, stand, flip of zen, hands to forehead, mouth, heart. Then we each found a spot to sit on the floor of the tiny room.

Kalu Rinpoche was sitting on a mattress resting on a wooden platform. This was not only where he slept, but also where he taught, meditated, performed his practices, and ate many of his meals. He was so thin, delicate, and ethereal, it seemed he might float away.

Being in that tiny room with Kalu Rinpoche was like floating in the middle of a huge, very still mountain lake, and being absorbed by the lake.

After everyone was seated, Kalu Rinpoche looked around the room with his deer eyes, then stopped, staring directly at me. Under his intense gaze, I shrank into my skin, certain he could see into my crazy, inferior, overly emotional mind. He waved his long delicate fingers over his porcelain teacup as he began speaking in his gentle whisper. His interpreter seated on the floor beside the bed translated, "Your minds are like a raging river. They must become still like the water in this teacup."

I sank into the openness of Kalu Rinpoche's presence. He was like a giant tuning fork and the cells of my body began to vibrate to the harmony of his being. As Rinpoche continued, the gentle murmur of his voice filled the room. When the translator began speaking, Kalu Rinpoche again looked directly at me. "All phenomena are merely a projection of your state of consciousness. Any appearance that arises, like the appearance in a dream, is merely a projection of your mind. If an enemy arises, you might want to kill that enemy."

This wasn't a teaching on Chenrezig practice. I stared at the floor. *Am I really thinking Palmo is my enemy? I certainly don't want to kill her. But I do want to* be *her–to be that gentle, steady, and composed.*

I returned my attention to Kalu Rinpoche. He was watching his translator who continued, "Indeed, you might even kill your enemy. But another will simply arise, because all appearances are simply a projection of your own state of consciousness."

Rinpoche focused on each person, one by one, with his loving gaze. I shifted on the hard floor. *Even if I could make Palmo disappear, would another "Palmo," someone who seems so much better than me, who has everything I want, arise as a projection of my own state of consciousness?*

Rinpoche then began his instruction on Chenrezig practice. I don't remember a bit of that. I also don't know if he was aware of my plea for help. But his words opened a new line of investigation. I started to question my previously unexamined imperative to control, to modify my outer circumstance in order to find peace.

My emotions have not disappeared; at times, the seas are still stormy. Yet I've come to see that every attempt to eradicate my emotional reactions–or to stop my mind–only fuels an internal war. Slowly, slowly, oh-so-slowly, my constricting conclusion that my thoughts and emotions were enemies needing to be banished began to loosen. I was discovering a capacity to recognize the flares of my shameful inferiority and prideful anger as partners in a dance–with plenty of room for the tango.

Even though I know this truth, I can lose sight of it. Yet with grace, every thought, every sensation, every emotion–the good and the bad–can be seen as another arising of unending, empty potentiality, of beckoning stillness. Like Kalu Rinpoche's presence, like the water in his teacup.

Chapter Thirteen

ÖSEL TENDZIN AND *SAMAYA*

I was one of five burgundy-clad nuns sitting in a row, our backs against the wall in Chögyam Trungpa Rinpoche's meditation center in downtown Los Angeles. We were waiting for Kalu Rinpoche to arrive. It had been six months since we returned from India. My life was now focused solely on preparing for the three-year retreat–doing my practices, chanting, learning Tibetan, cleaning houses. But then we learned that Kalu Rinpoche was coming to the States again, to Los Angeles. Due to his age and health, we knew our opportunities to see him were numbered. And since he wouldn't be visiting our monastery in New York, those of us not in retreat arranged to travel to L.A.

In the cab on the way to Chögyam Trungpa Rinpoche's center, Dechi quietly turned to face me. "Paldrom, do you know why Kalu Rinpoche agreed to come to Los Angeles?"

I shook my head no.

I'd certainly pondered the why–this trip was so unexpected–but my wondering had been overshadowed by delight. I was going to be in Kalu Rinpoche's presence again. The devotion I once showered on Dan now fully belonged to Kalu Rinpoche. This loving surrender was fostered by each of my practices as I repeatedly visualized the deity as a manifestation of my guru.

We sped past the billboards lining the L.A. freeway. Dechi took a deep breath, looking at her hands. "You know that before

Chögyam Trungpa Rinpoche died, he named one of his Western students, Ösel Tendzin, to be his Vajra Regent, his successor and lineage holder."

I nodded a yes.

Dechi paused as if carefully choosing what she wanted to say next. "Well, the Vajra Regent had sex with a number of his students, both men and women ... and he has AIDS. Even though he knew he was infected, he didn't use any protection. Apparently, he thought his realization would prevent him from spreading the virus. Of course, it didn't. And some of the people he had sex with got infected. One of them died."

I could only eke out, "Oh, my."

I stared out the dirty window at the traffic lights penetrating the smog, attempting to digest this information. I was thankful Kalu Rinpoche was my guru–and that Lama Norlha was the head of our monastery. *Lama can be challenging, but I'm glad he's so stubbornly traditional. He's a dinosaur for sure ... like a Tyrannosaurus rex.* I smiled, visualizing the fierce image.

When we arrived at the center, a greeter directed us to our seats–a line of cushions on the floor against the right-side wall of the meditation hall. Since Dechi held her nun's vows the longest, she took her seat at the head of the row. We settled in, careful to maintain a traditionally monastic demeanor. We each draped our zen across our left shoulder, the ends spread just so across our laps. Our right arms were bare in the room's chilly air.

More than fifty of Chögyam Trungpa Rinpoche's students sat on the floor facing the front of the large, dimly lit hall. Some sat cross-legged on firm rectangular or round meditation cushions, or on three-foot square cotton mats called *zabutons*. Others rested on six-inch tall wooden meditation benches with legs tucked under the benches, shins on the floor. A few sat in the back of the room on folding chairs.

Even though Chögyam Trungpa Rinpoche's students sat in proper meditation position, even though all were silent, the atmosphere was not calm or meditative. From my spot against the wall, I felt like an interloper as I watched the students waiting. My delight at once again being with Kalu Rinpoche was now layered with a fog of disbelief and sadness. I hoped Dechi's revelation about the Vajra Regent was just a rumor or an exaggeration but reminded myself that Kalu Rinpoche's decision to make this trip confirmed the gravity of the situation. He wouldn't have traveled from India just to quell a rumor.

After fifteen minutes of anxious silence, Kalu Rinpoche and a handful of Tibetan monks filed into the room and took their seats on cushions against the wall directly opposite us. I was surprised Trungpa Rinpoche's students hadn't provided a raised platform for Kalu Rinpoche. During all the ceremonies in Bodh Gaya, as well as for those at our monastery in New York, Kalu Rinpoche's seat had been elevated at least four feet from the floor, as it was traditionally done. But I reminded myself this was simply just another example of how Chögyam Trungpa Rinpoche (and now his students) had broken from tradition.

As I watched Kalu Rinpoche's E.T. eyes, my heart quietly relaxed, softening and warming a bit more with each breath. The room filled with the deep droning chanted tones of the monks' traditional opening prayers, then Kalu Rinpoche began to speak in his whispery Tibetan. One of the monks translated, "When the teacher gives the student instruction, a connection, a bond of *samaya* is formed. A promise is made. The teacher is committed to helping the student; the student is committed to following the instruction of the teacher. The student must maintain samaya by holding a pure view of the teacher, seeing all his actions as motivated only by a desire to benefit all sentient beings."

I first learned about the samaya bond between teacher and

student, about the importance of maintaining *dak nang*–a pure view of one's teacher–from Lama Norlha. The student creates a ring of receptiveness for the hook of the guru's teaching. Lama Norlha demonstrated this linking by holding his thick thumb and forefinger together to form an oval, then pulling on the oval with the bent forefinger of his other hand. He further illustrated the power of pure view with a traditional story he first heard as a child. I don't remember the exact words, but I'll share my best rendition of the tale. Each time he told it, he began with a tone of seriousness, but his eyes would twinkle in delight as he spoke the last few sentences.

The Tooth

> Many, many years ago a young man desperately wanted to travel to India, to the land of the Buddha, to find a teacher to provide instruction on the path to enlightenment. But this earnest young man didn't have the means to undertake his trip. His mother, seeing his pure desire, offered to fund the journey. The day he left, while thanking his mother, the young man asked what he could ever do to repay her kindness. She thought for a moment, and said, "Please bring me a small holy object from the land of Buddha. This will be enough."
>
> The young man traveled to India, found his teacher, received teachings, and with a full heart trekked back to his homeland in Tibet. However, it wasn't until he was only a day's journey from his home that he remembered his devoted mother's request. With overwhelming regret for his failure, he sat down on the ground and put his head in his hands. Auspiciously, in the dirt directly in front of him, he

> noticed the skull of a dog. Pulling one of the teeth from the dog's skull, he wrapped it in a scrap of red cloth and tucked it into his pocket.
>
> The next day, upon his return, he presented the tooth to his mother. "Dear Mother, I bring you this tooth from the Buddha himself."
>
> She was overcome with gratitude for the power of the Buddha's direct blessing contained in this holy relic. She placed it on her shrine and prayed to it each day. Her devotion, her pure view, was so unreserved that before the end of the month she attained nirvana, full Buddhahood.

The essence of those samaya teachings echoed as I continued watching Kalu Rinpoche. He lovingly gazed at Chögyam Trungpa Rinpoche's students as if viewing a field of magnificently blooming wildflowers blowing in a gentle breeze. I leaned back against the wall, ever so slightly, careful to maintain an appropriately dignified posture. *Ösel Tendzin destroyed the samaya bond. That's why Kalu Rinpoche traveled all this way. He's come to help straighten out this mess.*

The students glanced at each other as they waited for Kalu Rinpoche to continue. Finally, after several minutes of silence, through the translator, Kalu Rinpoche asked if anyone had questions. One student stood up stiffly. Her voice quivered with an intensity barely masking outrage, "The Vajra Regent has betrayed our trust. He needs to step down. He should be asked to resign."

Many of the students nodded in agreement.

I straightened my spine. *Yes, of course. Ösel Tendzin needs to step down. Maybe Rinpoche will offer a suggestion about a replacement.*

The translator began to relay Kalu Rinpoche's response. "If you've taken teachings or empowerments from the Vajra Regent, he is now your teacher."

A murmur ran through the room. Clearly many of these students had received both teachings and empowerments from Ösel Tendzin. He'd been functioning as a lineage holder for several years now, even prior to Chögyam Trungpa Rinpoche's death.

The translator continued, "You have a bond of samaya with the Vajra Regent. This bond must not be broken–no question. You must maintain your view that his actions are only for the benefit of all sentient beings."

A few students stood up and objected, attempting to find a way out of this seemingly ironclad interpretation of the samaya contract. I stared at Kalu Rinpoche. These students were cornered into an impossible dilemma–either break their samaya or suspend reason and values. How could Kalu Rinpoche require this? It seemed impossible. Could I view this dog's tooth as the Buddha's? Did Lama's tale reveal a cultural capacity, a norm, for this depth of surrender?

From my culture's story bank, I remembered how the White Queen had goaded Alice in Wonderland to believe the impossible. The Queen had officiously claimed to have believed as many as six impossible things before breakfast, but Alice had declined to try, even on the other side of the looking glass.

After the meeting ended, one of Kalu Rinpoche's monks ushered the five of us from New York into a small hallway behind the shrine room. At the end of the hall, Kalu Rinpoche was seated on a metal folding chair. One at a time, we walked down to sit at Kalu Rinpoche's feet for a few minutes. No translator was available, so for this second (and my last) private meeting with Kalu Rinpoche, I could only grin and nod. He gently smiled back as he patted the top of my head, over and over again.

That night as I drifted toward sleep, I melted into the nectar of Kalu Rinpoche's patting approval. Floating in a sea of devotion, I willed myself to suspend my judgment about Kalu Rinpoche's instruction to Chögyam Trungpa Rinpoche's students, to rest unfettered in unquestioning pure view.

The next day, I returned to our retreat center in New York and immediately looked for Lama Norlha. I had news to share with him before his flight to Los Angeles. Glowing with pride with my newfound capacity to maintain my pure view and my samaya bond with Kalu Rinpoche, I ran up the stairs and found him in the shrine room.

Breathlessly I began, "Lama, Chögyam Trungpa Rinpoche's students wanted Kalu Rinpoche to ask the Vajra Regent to step down. But Kalu Rinpoche didn't agree. He told them they had to maintain a pure view of the Vajra Regent because they have samaya with him."

Lama blinked and tilted his head before he frowned. "Kalu Rinpoche confused. He getting bad advice. No problem. I will explain to him."

He smiled and left the room. I stared at the space where he'd been standing.

What? Lama doesn't think his guru is infallible and perfect. He doesn't think everything Kalu Rinpoche says will benefit all sentient beings? What about Lama's pure view? What about his samaya?

Relief spread through me, as if a weight pressing on the cells of my body quietly faded away. *Maybe I don't have to will myself to believe impossible things.* I remembered the Buddha's instruction to not simply accept the teachings, but to test them out, to trust one's own experience.

Tibetan tradition recognizes the power of the passing of truth from teacher to student, then student becoming teacher and passing to student. But this process isn't simply a passing of knowledge, of wisdom–it's a transmission of a fundamental shift of perception.

The power of samaya, of pure view, of loving devotion, opens and protects the channel. A closed heart and mind can block. But receiving doesn't require blind faith. Nor even agreement. Simply openness.

I don't know if Lama Norlha ever had that conversation with Kalu Rinpoche about the Vajra Regent. And if he did, how Kalu Rinpoche responded. But the Vajra Regent didn't resign; he lived for about another year. After his death from AIDS, the scandal faded.

I'd lost the refuge of naïve devotion and initially felt unmoored. But, like a child riding her bike for the first time without training wheels, the freedom of gliding through the open air far surpassed the comforting safety of those training wheels.

Chapter Fourteen
NOT PALMO

A few minutes before five, with the sun slipping toward the banks of the Hudson, I strode across the monastery's parking lot toward the shrine room, flipping my zen across my shoulder. Dechi was standing in front of the main building, slowly, rhythmically ringing the gong as a call to puja. The ripples of deep sound waves penetrated the stillness of the late afternoon air. A half an hour earlier, I'd returned from cleaning two houses. I raced my little white Datsun pickup down the long dirt driveway, imagining my truck was flying over the potholes in the bumpy dirt road.

After returning to my room, I pulled off my navy knit pants and layered my sleeveless monastic vest, the tonga, over a mandarin-collared yellow cotton shirt–the one piece of my nun's attire I wore to my cleaning jobs. Even though the shirt fastened at one shoulder and under one arm with tiny bell-shaped brass buttons, it didn't appear to be monastic wear. I could tuck the crisp saffron cotton into the elastic waistband of my work pants. But the tonga vest, constructed using two shades of burgundy fabric, with wing-like flaps at the shoulders, was clearly a part of my robes.

The tongas worn by senior lamas or tulkus (like the Dalai Lama or the Karmapa) often have golden yellow cloth or sometimes ornate silk brocade for the front panels. But every tonga vest has the burgundy shoulder flaps trimmed with blue cord.

After securing the tonga at my waist with a large safety pin, I began wrapping myself into the skirt part of my robes, the *shamthap* that both men and women wear. With practice, I'd learned to fashion the tube of seven yards of fabric into a skirt in less than a minute. First, I pulled the tube of burgundy cloth over my head, careful not to step into it, which would dishonor the holiness of this representation of my vows. Once I had the fabric hanging over my shoulders, I began folding and lapping, creating a triple layer of cloth on each side of my body. Holding those layers in place with my elbows, I pleated the remaining fabric across my belly. Then, with my elbows pinned against my body, my lower arms held in a penguin-like fashion, I wrapped my belt around my waist to secure the folded layers. Finally, I flipped the fabric sticking up above my waistline over the top of my belt to create a cummerbund-like effect.

The shamthap design is practical–a true one-size-fits-all. By varying how much fabric folds over the belt, the skirt can be lengthened or shortened; by widening or narrowing the pleats, it can be loosened or tightened. So, if I gained or lost weight, it was easy to achieve a "tailored" fit.

My traditional monastic belt was a gift from Lama Norlha–a flat strip of thick woven saffron cotton, two inches wide, seventy-two inches long. In India, on the bus from Delhi to Bodh Gaya, Lama presented belts to the three of us planning to take vows. Then, as if imparting ancient secret wisdom, he demonstrated a twirling method for creating braid-like fringe on each end of our belts. Part of learning to dress properly had been remembering to tuck the fringe under my belt, so it didn't peek out.

When I met with Kalu Rinpoche in Bodh Gaya, per Lama Norlha's suggestion, I asked for special permission to forgo wearing monastic attire to my cleaning jobs. Lama encouraged us to maintain a low profile when we interfaced with the surrounding community. The monastery was located in a middle-class suburb of Poughkeepsie, New York. I suspected his interest in this discretion was motivated in part by a concern with the structures on the property—most would never have passed local building codes, including the building where I lived. However, we weren't the only monastics in the area. A Franciscan retreat center was directly across the street from the entrance to our driveway. Every now and then I glimpsed a friar walking along the road in his hooded long brown habit, belted with a white rope.

I appreciated having the special permission to wear Western clothing to my cleaning jobs. This helped me maintain a relatable, thus trustworthy, appearance. Many of my customers (including a mid-level IBM executive, an architect, a doctor, and a retired couple living in New York City with a weekend home in Poughkeepsie) entrusted me with a key to their front door. Usually, no one was home when I cleaned.

Working in these homes, with televisions, magazines, newspapers, radios, and central heating and air conditioning, sharply contrasted with my life at the monastery. Our buildings were warmed with woodstoves. In the heat of summer, we cooled ourselves with box fans propped on the windowsills. I slept and practiced in a tiny rustic room and chanted in a shrine room filled with intricate explosions of reds and golds. My companions had shaved heads and dressed in layers of burgundy fabric, their shamthaps wafting above the ankles as they walked.

The monks and nuns regularly shaved their heads, but I didn't. Still, I was careful to never let my hair grow longer than the regulation width of two fingers. I found a discount hair salon in a shopping mall to maintain my pixie cut—another way I straddled the line between living strictly as a nun and mingling in the Western world.

Even though jewelry was forbidden, I could wear my *gao*—a hollow silver pendant filled with tiny packets of blessed substances ready to be ingested as a quick blessing in the event of impending death. My gao, adorned with a Sanskrit seed syllable and suspended on a navy cord, bounced against my breastbone as I worked. Even though I was aware the gao is meant to serve as a reminder of impermanence, I treasured its jewelry-like beauty, only removing it to bathe or before going to sleep.

I didn't have the same attachment to my shamthap. Whenever I could get away with it, I pulled on my comfy navy stretch pants instead of the yards of burgundy fabric. I had ample opportunity for this minor rebellion—especially when Lama was traveling. I slipped into those pants when I was practicing in my room or even when I had some work to do around the center—basically whenever I wasn't going to the shrine room for chanting.

In this one way, I'd given up on striving for Palmo's perfection. She wore her robes like a dignitary dressed in a tuxedo, even when she was running around the property with a nail belt strapped over her perfectly folded shamthap, hammer in hand, or climbing up a ladder to build a shelf, or painting the shelf, or placing one of the thousand twelve-inch Buddhas on the ledge ringing the ceiling of the shrine room which, of course, she correctly called lhakhang.

She remained properly attired even when crouching on a scaffold to paint perfect Tibetan flower designs onto the walls. She appeared unflappable, always maintaining her placid exterior.

I pushed on the boundaries of proper monastic decorum in other ways, too. Rather than displaying a stoic peacefulness, I often couldn't control or even hide my emotions. It wasn't a rebellious choice. This was the impetus for my plea to Kalu Rinpoche on the hill in Sonada.

Even though I continued to remind myself of Kalu Rinpoche's teaching—"every arising is a projection of my own state of consciousness, like a dream"—comprehending, knowing, even believing his words hadn't removed my troubling emotions. But ... I began to watch them with a bit more curiosity. Still, I so wanted to stop the tight weight in my chest and the discomfort that gurgled in my belly each time I felt slighted or ignored by Lama. I did my best to fully inhabit the character of a surrendered nun, to mask my disappointed sadness or anger. At times I was successful.

My favorite chanting session was after the evening meal. Since I worked during the day, tidying the kitchen after dinner was my assignment—every single day. Even though I'd rush to transfer the leftover soup into a plastic container, wash the pot, put the soup and yogurt into the fridge and wipe the counters, Lama often began Chenrezig puja before I completed my tasks.

Many evenings, as I finished wiping down the sink, the sound of chanting drifted down the stairs. Kicking off my shoes, I rushed up the steps to the shrine room, my mind whirring with irritation. Sometimes, in these moments, I recalled the story of Martha, burdened with all the work, while her sister, Mary, sat at Jesus' feet. I slid onto my cushion, hiding my distress, while everyone remained focused on the chanting. By the time puja ended, the tightness in my chest and belly would dissipate, and I'd smile peacefully as we filed from the room.

However, there were other times when my peaceful-nun persona was impossible to maintain. When I learned that Palmo and Chodrin had surreptitiously been working with Lama to make arrangements to travel to India for a two-month course being offered by the Tibetan master, Khenpo Tsultrim Rinpoche, I repeatedly burst into tears in the dining room, and even during puja chanting.

Just a week prior to learning about their trip, I spotted Palmo and Chodrin in Chodrin's hatchback, driving away from the monastery. It was unusual for either of them to leave the monastery grounds, so I asked Lama where they were going. He replied, "Oh, some shopping."

When I discovered they actually were on their way to receive the vaccines needed for their trip to India, I ran directly to Lama's room to confront him. Standing in the doorway, my eyes flashed with anger and filled with tears, "Lama, you lied to me."

He stared at me for a brief moment before replying, "You must look at my intention."

I could only nod and sputter, "Oh, okay," as I watched him return his focus to his pechas. When he didn't look up again, I walked away.

Over the next several days, I couldn't stop my spiraling indignation. *Why didn't Lama–or Palmo, or Chodrin–let me know about this opportunity to study with Khenpo Tsultrim Rinpoche? They're going to get some vitally important teachings. And I won't. Not only that, Lama flat-out lied to me.*

I tried to maintain my pure view, my samaya, to discern Lama's compassionate motive in his seemingly effortless lie. Somehow, I needed to find a way to view this dog's tooth as the tooth of the Buddha. Once again, I was tossed into a tangle of nuances regarding the everyday application of our monastic vows. I'd accepted the reasoning that permitted the killing of roaches but avoided lingering in the logic that allowed eating meat from large animals, but not eggs.

Might Lama's relationship to lying be another example of differing cultural norms? Am I stuck in some Oklahoma Baptist black-and-white morality? Am I holding Lama to a higher moral standard than I apply to myself? It's not like I've never lied.

Lama had now shown me that nuances of interpretation exist even for the vow prohibiting lying. I suspected that perhaps he didn't want me to feel disappointed since I couldn't actually afford to go to India again–I needed to work so I could accumulate the funds to pay for my retreat. But his lie didn't remove my disappointment, only delayed it. And the secrecy amplified my experience of exclusion.

Wrestling with his justification, I recalled his reaction to Kalu Rinpoche's instruction regarding Ösel Tendzin and samaya. *Lama thought Kalu Rinpoche was confused. Maybe I can simply assume that Lama was confused. Maybe?*

After Palmo and Chodrin left for India, my disappointment faded. I continued my routine of cleaning, practicing, studying, and chanting. And I asked Drupten for extra Tibetan language tutoring so I could bolster my capacity to understand the practices we'd learn in retreat. To accelerate my saving, I accepted a job cleaning a small office building several nights each week.

Later that year, when Lama announced his plans for a trip to Tibet, I didn't even consider the possibility of tagging along. But Chodrin and Palmo both joined him on his six-month journey.

The day they returned, those of us who stayed behind gathered to welcome them home. We formed a loose circle in the large upstairs anteroom, standing on the amber carpeting I often vacuumed. Lama's giant battered suitcases rested unopened outside the door to his room. The sun filtered through the golden curtains onto the bright yellow walls, creating an extra softness and radiance. Someone asked about the nunnery they helped rebuild. Someone else asked about any difficulties they encountered in crossing the border. Another asked if they'd seen any yaks, the Tibetan long-haired bovine creatures that once roamed the Tibetan plateau.

Lama's eyes twinkled. "Yes. Palmo riding yak." His short legs created a wide tree trunk of stability and his chest expanded as he grinned and continued. "She liking very much. Inside she very happy. Outside showing nothing. Never see on her face how she feeling. Palmo like this. Good discipline. Never showing any happy-sad."

He smiled across the circle in Palmo's direction, then looked directly at me. "Paldrom, you need be more like this. More like Palmo. This very good qualities. Like Palmo."

I nodded, then blinked rapidly, attempting to waylay my tears. Luckily, someone asked about the Tibetan weather or about yak butter tea. Grateful for the distraction, I quietly backed out of the room.

A few days later when Lama asked to meet with me, I assumed he probably wanted to discuss my seriously under-developed poker face. Still I hoped he'd noticed that my chanting and drum playing had improved while he was away, so wanted to offer some private words of encouragement.

After Chenrezig puja, I followed Lama to his room and waited in the doorway. He began his daily task of emptying the water from the set of offering bowls lined up on his dresser. I waited. Focusing on drying one of the bowls, he began, "Maybe you doing some sitting meditation very good. Very helpful. Fifteen minutes two times every day."

I blinked. "Sitting meditation? But Lama, what about Ngöndro?" *Why does he want me to do that? I don't think he's requiring this of anyone else.* I pressed my tongue against the roof of my mouth and took a quick breath. *Don't start crying.*

"Lama, I tried sitting meditation before I came here. I wasn't very good at it. Maybe you could give me some instruction?" I adjusted my zen. This was my chance to receive some private teaching, like he was giving to Palmo when he asked her to come to his room.

Lama dried one of his bowls as he glanced in my direction. "No problem, I'm telling someone to teach you."

I nodded, attempting to appear grateful. There was nothing to say; I couldn't ignore a direct instruction from my teacher. Yet, I was certain he gave me this additional practice due to my less-than-stellar capacities.

The next day, I met with one of the nuns who'd completed the three-year retreat. We sat on a bench at the entrance of the main house, the overhang providing shade from the baking sun. Her instructions were brief. "You could focus on a candle, or on a picture, or maybe just watch your breath. That's probably best. Pay attention to your breath. And count to twenty-one. One count for each breath. When you reach twenty-one, begin again."

Much later I learned the seven points of proper meditation posture–the optimum positioning of legs, arms, back, eyes, jaw, mouth, tongue, and head–and the guidance to proceed gently without force. So, month after month, then year after year, I sat with my eyes closed, bringing my attention to my breath, attempting to focus on counting to twenty-one while watching my breath rise and fall.

Sometimes, I took a break at a cleaning job and leaned against a living room wall for fifteen minutes. Or I sat on the monastery bench overlooking the Hudson. Sometimes I sat in the shrine room or on my bed. I tried meditating first thing in the morning. I unsuccessfully attempted meditating at night right before going to sleep. For a while, I put the fifteen minutes back-to-back, thirty minutes at a time. Sometimes I couldn't maintain focus on my breath for longer than three seconds. Often, I fell asleep. Yet even though I felt woefully incompetent, even though time seemed to slow during those minutes, I persevered, because I'd received a direct instruction from my Lama.

One weekend, a young woman from Lama's center in New York City came for a visit. Lama asked me to work with her to prepare the raw plywood of the dining room floor for painting. Our task was to fill the small knotholes and imperfections with spackling, then sand those spots along with any other rough patches. So, on Friday after dinner, we lifted the twenty banquet-sized tables onto their sides, folded the metal legs, then leaned the tables against the wall under the same windows I'd cleaned in preparation for Kalu Rinpoche's visit.

Then, on Saturday morning we began spackling and sanding our way toward the kitchen. For hours on our hands and knees, we focused on one square foot at a time. The dusty scent of plywood dust rose from the floor.

Late Sunday afternoon, Lama materialized to inspect our efforts. We both scrambled to our feet in respect. Looking directly at the visitor, Lama nodded his approval. "So good. Such hard work. Thank you so much. Good, you coming here, working."

He approvingly patted her shoulder and she beamed, "Thanks, Lama."

Without a glance in my direction, he disappeared down the hallway. I returned to the expanse of plywood floor, to the square of sandpaper I'd left moments earlier. Just like so many times before, again I was flooded with my wish for approval, as if wearing a sandwich board that said, "Please Like Me." But this time there were no tears.

I stared at the empty hallway bringing my attention to the intensity of my desire for Lama's approval with a newfound sober curiosity. *My samaya requires that I view Lama's actions as only for the benefit of all sentient beings, including me.*

I turned my gaze to the row of glass-doored buffet cabinets against the dining room wall, filled with the plates, bowls, and lidded mugs reserved for visiting dignitaries. *I keep trying to pretzel myself into some version of an ideal nun so Lama will like me. But that's clearly not working. As hard as I try, I'm never going to be a model nun. Never a Palmo. Maybe Lama just doesn't have any idea how to deal with someone who's as emotionally stormy as me. He grew up in a monastery. Maybe emotions are just foreign to him. Or maybe he's strategically ignoring me because that's exactly what I need.*

I returned to my sanding. *The why doesn't matter. Kalu Rinpoche said everything is simply an arising, a manifestation, of my own state of consciousness—only my own state of consciousness. I can't get rid of my consciousness. And I can't seem to get rid of my emotions. All I can do is watch them, like watching my breath.*

That tiny toehold of openness began to melt the edges of the overwhelming intensity of my emotional reactions. There were plenty of opportunities for observation. Every time Lama started Chenrezig puja before I could make it into the room. Every time I watched his eyes soften as Palmo spoke at the dining table. Every time I waited for him to notice and applaud my precise and steady beating of the drum or my improving ability to keep up with the chanting. Watching these recurring impulses of internal distress, a pathway into an unknown capacity to observe, began to be revealed.

One day, after swabbing the toilet at one of my cleaning jobs, I noticed I was annoyed with the toilet for not flushing properly, thus prolonging my task. Like a movie running in slow motion, I watched first the flash of discomfort, instantly followed by a burst of irritation. The sensation was so familiar. My response had arisen unbidden, riding on the wave of perceived difficulty.

I laughed. I was angry with a toilet–an inanimate object. With this realization my breath slowed. A mind-stopping peace gently flowed from the center of my body out to my fingers and toes.

This moment of clarity didn't end the intensity of my emotional reactions. My longing, resentment, sadness, and anger did not disappear. All those emotions continued their rumblings like the troll under the bridge threatening to eat the Billy Goats Gruff. But finally, finally, the troll was becoming an ally, my teacher.

Chapter Fifteen

MERRILY, MERRILY, MERRILY, MERRILY

When I couldn't go to India with Palmo and Chodrin to study with Khenpo Tsultrim Rinpoche, I was certain I'd missed my one and only chance to receive his teachings. But I was wrong. The year after their trip, Lama invited Khenpo Tsultrim to our center to present a month-long course on *Mahamudra,* the core philosophy of Tibetan Buddhism. After the first teaching session, Drupten stopped several of us in the hallway. "We didn't learn anything like this in retreat. This is special. Pay attention."

Our practices focused on deity visualization, repeatedly creating alternative realities using the power of the imagination and loving devotion, then dissolving the alternative realities into emptiness. The text Khenpo Tsultrim was teaching utilized the power of logic, of reason, of thought. This method of investigation, developed and perfected for centuries by realized masters, delves into the nature of awareness, of our perceptions of reality–similar to the conceptual investigations of quantum physics. The teachings are like a guidebook, a map, for exploring beyond concept. Although studying a map is not actually taking the journey, facts, details, and descriptions can be helpful prior to traversing unknown territory.

Khenpo Tsultrim Rinpoche taught in the shrine room, seated on the same dais occupied by Kalu Rinpoche and Jamgon Kongtrul

Rinpoche during their visits. He'd earned the designation as a Rinpoche due to his realization. The title of Khenpo, analogous to PhD, was awarded after years of intensive study of Buddhist philosophy.

His pockmarked face had a fiercely peaceful assurance, unlike anything I'd ever seen or have seen since. I wondered if this reflected the years he spent meditating in graveyards. Each time he draped his fuchsia-toned zen across one shoulder, I pictured him sitting erect and alone in barren darkness.

As he read and then commented on the text, he looked over the top of his glasses and leaned slightly each time he turned toward his translator. I did my best to follow the written passages, to recognize the words of his spoken Tibetan, but struggled to comprehend the concepts–like interdependent origination, or the moment between thoughts, or the convergence of emptiness, bliss, and awareness.

The text cautioned that a glimpse of clarity is often overlooked–because it's so ordinary, so fleeting, so utterly natural. I believed I needed to stay sharp, to think more clearly, to try harder, so I could reason my way into understanding.

One sunny afternoon, in the sweltering summer heat, the box fans hummed. Khenpo Tsultrim's zen had slipped from his shoulder and now hung loosely at his waist. His voice boomed, then his translator gently transformed his Tibetan into English. My mind whirred with the Tibetan letters dancing on the page, the concepts floating in the air. Overwhelmed by my effort to understand, I closed my eyes and watched the flow of my labored thinking. With this silent observing I somehow stumbled into an awareness closer than thought, an ever-present ground of still clarity. The moment was unexpectedly ordinary, yet extraordinary. All I could do, all I wanted to do, was lean against the wall and melt into the embracing stillness–a stillness like the tranquil peaceful silence of Kalu Rinpoche's room.

For the next two weeks, I attended as many of Khenpo Tsultrim's sessions as possible without jeopardizing my cleaning jobs. I imagined I could somehow recapture the blissful stillness, recreate the moment, unaware of the futility of that effort. I didn't recognize the cracking, but a brick or two had loosened in my wall of solid reality. When the teachings ended, I stored my many pages of scribbled notes on a shelf in my room and returned to my routine.

A few months later, after the nights of sleeping with a fan were replaced by a fire in the woodstove and snuggling in my sleeping bag, I pulled myself out of bed in the pre-dawn stillness. As I padded across the parking lot on my way to puja, the gravel driveway crunched under my footsteps. When I reached the apron in front of the main building, the barely perceptible flap of my shoes on concrete mingled with a ting-ting, ting-ting, ting-ting–the gentle sound of Lama's *tingshas* wafting from his window. He was performing a practice called *Cho Tor*, ringing his pair of three-inch meditation cymbals.

Just for an instant or two, with the ting-ting of Lama's tingshas, reality cracked. This was not an intellectual understanding. Not a believing, but a knowing, penetrating reason. I was in a dream. Merrily, merrily, merrily, merrily. My very me-ness was as the Mahamudra text had described–a mirage, a story, a dream.

I don't know if the gift of this moment was a further unfolding of the awareness invoked by Khenpo Tsultrim's teaching in the shrine room. Or if all those fifteen-minute stretches of bringing my focus to my breath again and again had created a new neural pathway. Or maybe it was grace. Or maybe some combination of all of those. Or none of them.

Like in Star Trek's holodeck, when the ship's computer experiences technical difficulty and segments of the fantasy world blink and falter momentarily revealing the holographic illusion, my mental programming wavered. Then it quickly booted back up. For three steps across the concrete, I was in a dream. Then ordinary awareness returned.

Poets and mystics have described the luminous knowing of the liminal borderland beyond the naked mind where facts and reason disintegrate and fail. Perhaps because my conceptual scaffolding was so shaped by the fairytales of my youth, I'll attempt to describe this wordless experience with a fairytale.

A Forest Dream

Once upon a time, not so long ago, a girl awoke to find herself already deep in a forest, as if she had been walking there forever. In a proper fairy tale, she would be a princess. But since this is not a proper fairy tale, she was not.

She didn't know why she was in this forest, couldn't recall a time before this forest-walking. As she gazed at her porcelain hands, the leaves rustled in the gentle breeze. The birds chirped as the morning sunlight filtered through the canopy of trees, casting shadows.

But suddenly the sun disappeared. Wind swept her hair about her face. She tightened her velvet wrap, fearful of something she couldn't name or even imagine. No more than she knew how she had appeared in these woods, did she understand the lurking danger. She only knew it was something bad. Her apprehension grew with each footstep.

Then, somewhere in the distance she heard a ringing, a quiet ting-ting of small cymbals. Instantly she knew she was not walking in a magical forest. It was a

> dream, a trance. Yet here she was, still in a forest, still observing her fearful self.
>
> In the next instant she opened her eyes and discovered she was sitting on her meditation mat in front of her beloved teacher. He was smiling and asked, "Which one is the real you? Who is aware of this you? Is there a real you?"

The momentary experience of the dream-like nature of reality didn't last. I was still Paldrom. Still subject to insecurity and comparison. My day-to-day life continued to feel just as solid and real as it always had. Yet for just a few moments, a veil had lifted.

New questions arose. *If I'm not who I believe myself to be, if I'm in a dream, then what about my emotions, my thoughts, my memories, projections, desires, likes, and dislikes?*

I was now even more determined to enter the three-year retreat so I could find a way to recapture this state of still awareness, to be like a perpetually meditating guru on a mountaintop. I didn't yet understand the folly of chasing after an experience. Didn't understand that every experience is temporary. That the glimpse is a side effect. Years later, I'd finally begin to understand the guidance to live one's life in devotion to a glimpse—even if there's never another one.

Chapter Sixteen
YOU'RE NOT *VAJRAYOGINI*

Months became years, and little or no social interaction was the norm. Each weekday morning after chanting, I grabbed my lunch reserved in the fridge, made my portable breakfast (peanut butter and strawberry jam between two pieces of toast), strode to my room, changed into my navy pants, then headed out to my cleaning jobs while nibbling on my sandwich. After work I returned to the monastery, went to my room to quickly change back into my robes, then back to the shrine room for evening chanting. This was followed by a quick dinner (a bowl of yogurt with jam), cleaning the kitchen, returning to the shrine room for Chenrezig puja, and finally to my room for some practice, study, and sleep.

Three nights a week, I skipped Chenrezig puja to drive a few miles to a local construction company's office building where I vacuumed, dusted, and emptied trash cans. Even though I was usually alone while cleaning during the day, and alone again when cleaning the office, when I could, I joined Drupten, Chodrin, and Palmo to practice spoken Tibetan. My ability to read and understand the Tibetan texts was improving, but my conversational Tibetan hadn't progressed much beyond the basics, of "How are you?" and "What's your name?"

I connected with other humans primarily during puja, our voices blending into one stream. Especially during the slower Chenrezig puja, I was often transported into Chenrezig's realm, much like when I was in grade school and caught up in reading Nancy Drew, or later, when becoming a character onstage.

Lama Norlha led the chanting, except when he was traveling. Even during the more rapidly chanted pujas, catching the wave of alternative reality was easier when he was in the room. I closed my eyes, rocking to the rhythmic drone of our voices as I beat the large round drum, hung in its shiny, red-lacquered wooden frame. Holding the mallet gently, I matched the tap-tap beat set by Lama's cymbals.

I wasn't able to play any of the horns. Even though I tried, I couldn't master the necessary skill of *oo-kor*, circular breathing, the same method used by Australian Aboriginal peoples to maintain a continuous flow of sound when playing the didgeridoo. I so wanted to play the oboe-like gyaling and the deep rumbling rag-dung horn. For weeks I attempted to master oo-kor using the time-tested training method of blowing into a straw in a glass of water, working to sustain a steady stream of bubbles. Drupten, a master on the horns, taught oo-kor to both Chodrin and Palmo using this method. But after weeks of continuous failure, I concluded that circular breathing was going to remain out of my grasp.

The one time I attempted to play the rag-dung horn during puja, trying to follow Dechi's lead, I not only could not sustain the notes using oo kor, but the results of my efforts were closer to a backfiring car than the sustained om-like tones. Dechi glared in my direction with a look of horror, like I was murdering the music. Lama continued playing the cymbals as he glanced in my direction. I noticed that his side-eye was accompanied by the slightest upturn in the edges of his mouth.

In time, I was able to serve as second on the cymbals—the flat *silnyen* and the more bulbous *rolmo*—accompanying Lama, or in Lama's absence, Drupten. Lama regularly cautioned, "No doing like this," as he held both cymbals together, mirroring one another. "Hitting together like this, definitely breaking."

Resting the cymbals in my lap, I tapped the beat while we chanted, matching Lama's lead. Then, as the horns thundered and squealed, I raised the cymbals–always careful to maintain their staggered alignment–and forcefully hit them together. Finally, I'd hold the cymbals lightly against each other as they continued to vibrate, allowing the waves of sound to continue and fade, like the ripples in water after a rock has broken the still surface.

As we chanted, I often pictured Trinley and the nuns in the retreat house also chanting in their second-story shrine room. After puja, walking across the parking lot toward my room, I eyed the windows of their shrine room peeking above the stockade fence. I hadn't heard from Trinley since the first few months of her retreat, but I understood she was focused on her meditation and practice. She'd gone inward. I had too.

I imagined living behind that stockade fencing where I'd finally learn the practices taught in retreat–practices for which I twice received empowerments from Kalu Rinpoche–including dream yoga (transforming ourselves in our dreams), clear-light yoga, illusory body, *Bardo* (yoga of the intermediate state), *Phowa* (transfer of consciousness to a pure Buddha-field at the time of death), and *Tummo* (generating heat to raise one's internal body temperature). When I came across a book in the center's library describing scientific accounts of yogis who could raise their body temperature by as much as twelve degrees during Tummo practice, I pictured Kalu Rinpoche meditating in a Himalayan cave during a winter storm.

One weekend at lunch, during the last year of Trinley's retreat, after Lama returned from one of his regular visits to the retreat houses, he began sharing about retreats in Tibet and the practice of Tummo. Seated at the head of the table, his eyes gleaming, he described how the retreating monks had been tested on their

Tummo proficiency. They were required to produce steam from wet sheets wrapped around their naked torsos while they meditated in the cold mountain air. I stared out the dining room windows, imagining Trinley wrapped in wet sheets. *She's a great meditator; she'll probably be able to produce steam after her years in retreat. But what about me? Will I be able to do that?*

Before I could wander further into my fantasy, Lama laughingly explained that Westerners weren't required to prove their Tummo capacity in this way. My vision of Trinley (and me) wrapped in wet sheets melted into emptiness, like the visualizations at the end of each practice. I didn't allow my face to show my relief.

By the time I finally started the fourth preliminary practice of Ngöndro–Guru Yoga–I was confident I was going to be able to take part in the next retreat. With prostrations, my body had surrendered again and again. Then I'd focused on purifying negative karma by repeating Dorje Sempa's mantra and filling myself with his cleansing light. After I finished this second part of Ngöndro (months after Palmo), I tackled the third segment, mandala offerings. With this, I accumulated merit, making offerings to all manifestations of enlightened mind, the Lamas, Buddhas, Bodhisattvas, and protectors and guardians of the Dharma.

The mandala practice is a symbolic ritual offering made by dropping small handfuls of uncooked white rice mixed with sparkly beads and faux pearls (representing gems) onto a slightly domed copper plate, then sweeping the mixture off the plate. Placing and sweeping, over and over again, while chanting the mandala prayer 111,111 times.

After months of sitting and repeating Dorje Sempa's mantra while also sitting to meditate for fifteen minutes twice each day, I'd welcomed this more physically engaging practice. The beauty of the gleaming copper plate and glistening baubles, the feel of the smooth rice as it flowed against my palm, the sound of the rice hitting the copper, all soothingly filled time, like sitting by a trickling mountain stream. The chanted prayer for the mandala practice is shorter than Dorje Sempa's mantra, so I was able to complete the required recitations in just a couple of months. Then I could finally start working on the last preliminary practice–Guru Yoga.

For this fourth part of Ngöndro, the practitioner visualizes becoming the female deity, Vajrayogini, possessing the essence of all the Buddhas. Enlisting my acting skills of immersing myself into a character's mind, body, and emotions, I closed my eyes while chanting Vajrayogini's prayer. I imagined myself naked with unbound flowing hair and blood-red skin, adorned with bone ornaments, and standing on one leg in the center of a blazing fire, baring my fanged teeth and laughing. As Vajrayogini, in one hand I held a curved knife representing the removal of all defilements. In the other hand, I cradled a skull cup filled with the nectar of *mahasukha*, "the great bliss."

The first three Ngöndro practices–prostrations, chanting Dorje Sempa's mantra, and dropping rice and jewels on a copper plate–were all departures from any kind of religious ritual I'd previously encountered. But when I began visualizing myself as Vajrayogini, I was surprised to recognize a few tendrils of those Baptist sermons. Wrathful Vajrayogini looked a lot like a hellish demon. Yet as I settled into her blood-red skin, I melted into her fierce presence–an uncompromising expression of loving compassion.

Visualizing myself as Vajrayogini, I repeated her prayer–a request for three specific qualities of enlightenment. First, she asks to recognize the body as the physical manifestation of a Buddha in time and space. Second, to see energy as the luminous form of clear light attained upon reaching the highest dimensions of practice. And finally, she requests recognition of the mind as the unmanifest, inconceivable aspect of Buddha nature out of which all Buddhas arise and to which they return after their dissolution. It's a big ask—for full and complete enlightenment.

Again and again, I chanted these requests, merging into Vajrayogini's fierce fullness. Acting had taught me to imagine a backstory, to search for the "why" beneath a character's words and actions. Now using those same skills of imagination and embodiment I was stepping into Vajrayogini's world. After several months of repeating her prayer, I began to wonder why Vajrayogini would be praying for a realization she already possessed. I reasoned that she might pray for all sentient beings to be granted liberation, but couldn't reconcile why this embodiment of the essence of enlightenment needed to pray for the qualities of enlightenment.

I attempted to dismiss my concern. To just chant. To not think. But my quandary remained, so, one evening after puja, I stopped by Lama's room.

"Lama, I'm having a hard time with my Guru Yoga practice. When I visualize myself as Vajrayogini, why am I praying for the qualities of enlightenment I already possess?"

As I stood in the doorway, he looked at me with raised eyebrows, "But you're not Vajrayogini, are you?"

"No," I quietly muttered as I shook my head. I waited for a few minutes, but he closed his eyes, his lips moving with his mantra repetitions, the beads of his mala quietly clicking as they passed through his fingers. I dared not speak my thoughts.

Did Lama not understand my question? I know I'm not Vajrayogini, I'm Paldrom. But isn't the instruction to imagine I'm her, to become Vajrayogini in the same way I become Chenrezig or Tara when we chant those practices? How can I imagine that I am Vajrayogini and not Vajrayogini at the same time? And if I am Vajrayogini, why do I need to pray for enlightenment?

When he didn't look up again, I backed out of the room.

For the next several days, each time I attempted to repeat

Vajrayogini's prayer, I could only focus on the inconsistency. I dared not ask about it again, so attempted to think outside my rational logic. But I just couldn't find a way to both visualize myself as Vajrayogini while repeating her prayer. I could not dissolve my mind's black-and-white analysis, could not simply allow the paradox.

I so wanted to be a successful nun, even though I continued to avoid wearing the yards and yards of my shamthap whenever possible. But now, faced with this dilemma, I concluded my best option was to simply skip this fourth segment of Ngöndro. This was more than a minor rebellion. I knew if I consulted with Lama about my decision, he'd never condone it, and then my samaya would require me to comply. So, I decided to never ask.

I justified my decision. This allowed more time to prepare for retreat. I could now work on memorizing the rapid, complicated sections of our daily chanting–the same pujas we'd chant every day in retreat. Then, when chanting, I could melt into the visualizations. And I had more time to study Tibetan, to look up the words of our texts in my black leather-bound Tibetan dictionary with tissue-thin pages.

I was certain Lama wouldn't notice that I'd stopped doing this last segment of Ngöndro. He never asked about my progress. In one of my notebooks, I scribbled, "Lama is ignoring me more and more and it's okay." I was beginning to find my own way, to not blindly fall into that familiar longing for Lama's approval, to follow the breadcrumbs of a way illuminated by a fierce surety–like Vajrayogini's.

Chapter Seventeen
FOUR THOUGHTS THAT TURN THE MIND TO DHARMA

It had been more than five years since Lama first suggested I stay at the monastery, and a year and a half since the end of Trinley's three-year retreat. Now, in less than a week, I was going to begin my own. As I entered the women's retreat house, Lama was waiting for me next to the woodstove, the only source of heat for the building. Although dormant, its sweet, smoky scent lingered in the July warmth. I was finally going to learn which of the nine doors opening onto this central area led to my room—the room I'd live in for at least the next three years, three months, and three days. For the first time since I helped Dechi tape and spackle the kitchen, I was allowed inside the tall stockade-fenced retreat grounds.

Minutes earlier, I hurried down the hill. *Which room will I get? Will Lama give me Trinley's room?* Trinley had wanted to be a participant in this retreat, her second, but when Lama denied her request, she returned to the nearby Tibetan monastery in Woodstock. For the past year and a half, since her retreat had ended, we'd only spoken a few times. Rather than my pal from Oklahoma, she was now another nun on the path to enlightenment. She'd always been quiet and reserved, but now had no interest in chatting or fraternizing. Her focus was only on her practices. I'd changed too. The waves of my desire to socialize had diminished to barely noticeable blips.

I wasn't sure I wanted Trinley's room since it bordered Tsupa's.

Only a thin layer of sheetrock separated the rooms and during the last retreat, Tsupa had been irritated with the volume of Trinley's mantra repetitions. I didn't want to risk also annoying Lama's star student, the nun who helped build the retreat houses. This would be her third retreat, so she wouldn't join us for our daily pujas, but would practice her individually designed program in the same front corner room where she'd lived for many years, a room filled with sunlight from windows on two walls.

Lama had already assigned several of the rooms. Palmo was given the corner room mirroring Tsupa's. Chodrin would occupy the room next to the dining room where we'd gather for lunch each day. Its two-foot-tall dining table could accommodate floor seating for all nine retreatants and Lama. A nun who was participating in exchange for serving as our cook was assigned the room adjacent to the front door–the room closest to the open-air entry vestibule where our food and supplies would be delivered.

When I reached the burgundy door leading into the small vestibule, I gingerly turned the brass handle and stepped inside. Standing between the outside world and the land of retreat, momentarily enclosed in liminal space, I paused in the silence, noting the earth under my feet, the cloudless sky, the faint scent of pine, and the unpainted door before me.

Opening the next door, I stepped into the stillness of the dusty yard surrounded by stockade fencing. As I approached the retreat house, I noticed a single bench resting in the dirt and the scruffy weeds. Soon this yard would be the only outdoors to which I'd have access. After climbing two stairs to a small wooden landing, I pulled on the screen door and entered the quiet sanctity of the retreat house.

As my eyes adjusted, Lama came into focus, his brown leather loafers planted on the wooden floor. He was beaming as he wiped a bit of sweat from his forehead and gestured to the door directly behind him. "This room so good for you. So much warm in winter. So close to woodstove."

He was pointing to a room on the back of the house with one north-facing window. The room overlooking the outhouse. The room abandoned by its previous inhabitant, the nun I encountered at Chögyam Trungpa Rinpoche's cremation.

I took a step toward the open door, not allowing my face to show even a trace of the wave of deflation restricting my breath. I instantly willed a cheerful thought. *At least I'll have quick access to the outhouse ... and the shower.*

My new room bordered a short hallway leading to the rear entrance. Across the hall, a doorway led into a linoleum-floored room containing an acrylic shower stall fragranced by a bar of Zest soap and the industrial-sized plastic sink we'd use to wash our clothes.

I glanced at the woodstove, then at the doors to each of the rooms, unable to discern a noticeable distance from the stove to any of them. Lama walked over to the side of my doorway. I knew he wouldn't go in since entrance to the retreat rooms was restricted to its current occupant.

As I stepped into my nine-by-nine-foot room for the first time, I surveyed the white walls and plywood floor painted a deep burgundy. My gaze fell to the three-foot-square meditation box pushed into the corner closest to the doorway. It was constructed of raw unpainted pieces of plywood, open on top, waiting for me to climb in. The front and sides were three feet tall, the back, five feet. This was where I was going to spend most of my time–performing my practices, repeating mantras, meditating, eating breakfast and dinner, and attempting to sleep while sitting upright and cross-legged.

Lama glanced through the doorway. "Best you putting your box under the window. Sunlight coming in there. So good. So healthy."

He was right. The corner on the far side of the room under the north-facing window was the best location for my box. To my right, I noted the room's ruby-red enamel wooden shrine structure. If I put my box in the corner as Lama suggested, it would face the shrine. The only other object in the dim room was a four-foot-tall, six-inch-wide raw plywood bench–a shelf to place in front of my box. It would hold my chanting pechas and sometimes a cup of tea. At breakfast time, it would serve as a table for my bowl of hot cereal. In the evening, my soup.

The next day, Tsupa helped load my possessions into the back of the monastery's pickup truck. We took a bumpy ride down the hill, then she helped carry my worldly goods to the doorway of my new room. After she left, I slid my cot-sized futon next to my box and placed my prostration board against one wall. Then I pushed the trunk I'd brought from Minnesota into the room. I'd filled it with a three-year supply of necessities including votive candles, incense, assorted teas, small spiral-bound notebooks, pens, pencils, toothpaste, toothbrushes, and tampons.

Next, I scooted my K-Mart particle-board wardrobe into the room. I pulled out my robes and arranged them on the top shelf of the wardrobe cabinet. Then I unpacked a shiny new Farberware coffee pot (recommended by previous retreatants for warming tea water) and my new jumbo-sized sleeping bag, rated for zero-to-twenty-degree temperatures. I'd studied the L.L. Bean catalog to find one that would fully zip while seated upright with crossed legs.

In the silence of the empty retreat house, I sawed my futon in half with a serrated knife from the kitchen. The half futon exactly fit the bottom of my meditation box. I placed the remaining half next to the woodstove, certain one of my fellow retreatants would claim it to pad the bottom of her box.

Finally, I set up my shrine, placing my photos of Kalu Rinpoche behind seven carefully aligned stainless steel offering bowls. Lama had recommended purchasing them when we were in India. I filled each bowl with water, just to the edge, then arranged my reference books, including my black leather-bound Tibetan-English dictionary, onto one of the lower shelves of my shrine.

When Trinley's retreat started, Kalu Rinpoche had led a grand ceremony. The monks and nuns wore their finest woolen shamthaps, tongas, and zens, and donned ceremonial headwear—ruby red crown-like hats a foot tall, adorned with golden brocade. They marched single file into the retreat house enclosures, accompanied by the wailing of gyaling horns and waving of long thick sticks of incense.

Since Kalu Rinpoche was no longer alive and no other high lamas of our lineage were available, our retreat began with no pomp and circumstance. On a hot July morning three days after we moved in, Lama chanted some prayers, thereby officially sealing us into our cloistered abode. Retreat had begun.

SCHEDULE:

4:00 a.m.	Wake up
4:15-6:00	Practice session
6:00-8:00	Group chanting in lhakhang
8:00-8:20	Breakfast in room
8:20-noon	Practice session
Noon-2:00	Lunch in dining room, then free time
2:00-5:00	Practice session
5:00-7:00	Group chanting in lhakhang
7:00-7:15	Dinner in room
7:15-9:50	Practice session
9:50-10:00	Prepare for sleep
10:00 p.m.	Sleep

Ten hours, the bulk of our days, were allocated to our solitary practices, with four hours for group puja chanting. Before breakfast and dinner, we gathered upstairs in the shrine room to chant the same pujas performed during those hours in the men's retreat house and the main house shrine room. However, in the retreat houses we didn't chant Chenrezig puja after dinner. Those hours were designated for the day's fourth individual practice session.

During puja, two nuns at a time served as *chöpons*, rotating on a weekly basis. Each morning the two designated chöpons, rather than joining the chanting, filled the shrine room's hundreds of palm-sized metal offering bowls with water. We carried the water up the stairs in ten-gallon buckets, placing them on the plastic carpet protector in front of the shrine. Then we dipped a plastic pitcher into the bucket and carefully filled each bowl to the brim. In the late afternoon, we emptied the water back into the plastic buckets, dried each bowl, then lugged the buckets down the stairs and into the yard where we poured the used water into the dirt.

Every day, each chöpon polished one set of seven copper, brass, or silver offering bowls. We slipped on yellow plastic gloves to protect our hands from the harsh metal polish and tied cotton scarves over our mouths and noses. Our bandito-like masking not only shielded our lungs from the pungent chemicals of the polish, but also protected the bowls from our impure human breath. I was grateful that Lama had recommended purchasing stainless-steel offering bowls for my room's shrine so I didn't have to spend time polishing them during our limited unstructured time.

After waking up at four a.m., we had fifteen minutes to fill our water bowls and take care of our morning toiletry needs–without leaving our rooms. We each had a lidded ten-gallon white plastic bucket–like the ones we used to carry water to and from the lhakhang–to serve as a chamber pot during the hours we were confined. We were only allowed to exit our rooms to file up the stairs to the lhakhang for the morning and late afternoon puja chanting sessions, to go to the dining room for lunch, and during our free time after lunch. This was when we could access the outhouse, walk in the yard, take a shower, wash our clothes in the laundry sink and hang them on the clothesline strung from the side of the outhouse, or rest. After our evening solo practice session, we had ten minutes to empty and dry our water bowls and prepare for sleep.

For the first five weeks of the retreat, we didn't have to accumulate mantra repetitions. We'd been advised to enjoy the luxurious spaciousness, the simplicity, of those first weeks. Week one, our only assignment was to sit in meditation. Week two, we began contemplating the ordinary preliminaries: the Four Thoughts That Turn the Mind to Dharma. One thought each week.

I'd chanted the words of these Tibetan precepts at least once each day for almost five years now–with some comprehension. However, I'd never stopped to consider their deeper meaning, nor their implications. But now, in my humid, summery room, contained by my meditation box, my sole task was to focus on these statements meant to inspire diligence and focus.

I knew that after the first five weeks, we'd once again be tasked with completing the extraordinary preliminaries, the four practices of Ngöndro, beginning with another set of 111,111 prostrations. Then, finally, we'd begin to receive instructions on the practices taught only inside retreat. Although I'd previously abandoned the fourth segment of Ngöndro, Guru Yoga, I optimistically planned to ignore the illogical nature of Vajrayogini's prayer by focusing on my devotion to Kalu Rinpoche and my desire to become enlightened ... for the benefit of all sentient beings. However, long before the time to practice Guru Yoga arrived, I stumbled into a new thicket of thorny dilemmas. During the spaciousness of the weeks spent contemplating the Four Thoughts, my questioning mind would not be quiet.

The Four Thoughts are meant to serve as a reminder of the unique opportunity to escape from the wheel of *samsara*, the endless cycle of death followed by rebirth into one of the six realms: as a god, a jealous god, a human, an animal, a hungry ghost, or into one of the unbearably cold or hot hell realms. Transcending this cycle is nirvana, enlightenment.

The human realm is the only one of the six providing an escape hatch, a just-right Goldilocks zone offering the possibility of enlightenment. In the human realm, encountering the teachings of the Buddha is discovering a guidebook to transcendence. And participating in a three-year retreat and receiving instruction in the advanced esoteric methods is said to be as extraordinary as the appearance of a daytime star or a summer snowflake. To not take full advantage of this rare opportunity is compared to journeying to a land of wish-fulfilling gems and returning empty-handed.

In tiny letters penciled in one of my spiral-bound notebooks, I summarized the essence of the Four Thoughts That Turn the Mind to Dharma:

1. Precious human existence–This lifetime is a sterling opportunity I might not have again for millions of lifetimes.
2. Death and impermanence– I could die at any moment and lose the opportunity.
3. Karma– The bad things I've done in this and other lifetimes will catch up with me, causing reincarnation into realms far worse than this one.
4. Suffering of samsara– As long as I'm in samsara, I will suffer. Any pleasure I might experience is like the feast offered by the executioner.

As I read and re-read these words, my mind didn't turn in the direction the practice intended. With each passing week, rather than deepening in resolve, I bristled, noting the same quality of fear-inducing threat of future suffering I'd encountered in the Baptists' descriptions of eternal hell and damnation. I couldn't find the deeper truth hiding in the Four Thoughts. This opened a new cascade of doubt. Not even a hint of the peaceful stillness of Kalu Rinpoche's room was available, nor of Khenpo Tsultrim's teaching in the shrine room, or the dream-like nature of reality I'd briefly glimpsed on the gravel driveway.

I stared out my window, at the grayed slats of the stockade fencing, the dirt yard, the empty clothesline hung with weathered wooden clothespins, the tree next to the outhouse, the cloudless summer sky, willing myself to find a way to rectify my rebellious doubts and questioning. *What's wrong with me? Why can't I just be motivated by these Four Thoughts like everyone else?*

I pulled out the reference books I'd stashed on the shelves of my shrine and found supporting factors for each of the Four Thoughts. I copied the Eight Unfavorable Conditions, the Ten Opportunities, and the Twelve Links of Dependent Origination into one of my spiral notebooks. I pored through two of Chögyam Trungpa Rinpoche's books, looking to his more Westernized description of the Tibetan Buddhist paradigms and cosmology. Still, my uncertainty spiraled.

I stared out my window at the high fence. *Why do I have to question everything? Is that why Lama gave me this room with little sunlight and a view of the outhouse, a room abandoned by its previous inhabitant? What if he believes I'm not capable of achieving enlightenment? What if I'm not?*

I so longed for enlightenment to escape my emotional intensity, yet my desire for personal freedom had begun to soften. For the past five years, every practice session ended with dedicating any accumulated merit to the benefit of all sentient beings. Initially this was a rote exercise. But now a budding bodhisattva intention–the promise to be the last to go, to not pass into nirvana until every other sentient being had first been freed–had begun to temper my desperate grasping for personal escape.

Confined in the silence of my retreat room, I wondered if my intent to free myself from samsara was out of alignment with my Bodhisattva vow to not pass into nirvana until everyone else had been saved first. Maybe I needed to focus on service rather than personal enlightenment. This seemed like a legitimate avenue of investigation, something I could discuss with Lama. I dared not ask him about my misgivings regarding the tactics of the Four Thoughts. That line of inquiry needed to remain in my spiral notebooks, within the walls of my retreat room.

Later that week we were offered the opportunity to meet privately with Lama. So, after lunch, I climbed the stairs to the shrine room where he was waiting. I performed three prostrations, then sat down on the carpet in front of him.

"Lama, I'm concerned I'm not honoring my Bodhisattva vow by focusing on trying to become enlightened. Maybe that's being selfish. I'm not being in service to anyone."

He nodded, then smiled, "But you're not enlightened, so no really helping. First practice here in retreat. This very good. Then service."

That seemed valid. I returned to my room with a new resolve. *It's okay to focus on doing the practices, on becoming enlightened.*

I returned to my notes looking for further inspiration for my new resolve. I'd copied a passage from Chögyam Trungpa's *The Myth of Freedom*: "If we can make friends with ourselves, if we are willing to be what we are without hating parts of ourselves and trying to hide them, then we can begin to open to others. And if we can begin to open without always having to protect ourselves, then perhaps we can begin to really help others."

One afternoon, in the warm August stillness, weary from thinking, discerning, and studying, I leaned against the wall under my open window looking through the teeny squares of the screen and noticed Palmo silently digging a trench in the yard behind the kitchen. Lama was standing close by, directing, observing. I surmised there was some issue with the kitchen's plumbing.

Just an hour earlier, we'd gathered in front of the retreat house during our lunch break to meet with Lama. We sat around him on the dirt as he rested his outstretched arm on the backrest of the wooden bench. Palmo nestled at his feet and leaned her head against his knee. As he patted her head, I once again observed my familiar longing to be as accepted, as loved, as she seemed to be.

But now, after these weeks of sitting in my box–sorting, meditating, wrestling with the thoughts that had not turned my mind to Dharma–as I watched Palmo digging in the yard, I was enveloped by a new depth of dispassionate detachment. The letters of the words written in my notebooks had grown smaller and smaller. My breath was slower. Even my cells seemed more relaxed. The scene of Lama with Palmo appeared dreamlike, as if watching a slow-motion black and white movie. She was outside in the sunlight, with Lama, while the rest of us were confined to our rooms. Lama had again picked only her.

Watching her dig in the dirt, I saw the roots of seeking planted so many years earlier–the longing to belong, the yearning for acceptance. As she silently pushed the shovel into the ground then lifted mounds of dirt, my thoughts slowly paraded. *I can simply allow this desire. I don't need to hate this part of myself. I don't need to change it. I don't need to become Palmo. In fact, I truly don't want to. She's tied to Lama. I'm free.*

In that moment I knew I could surrender to imperfectly practicing in my little room in the back of the house. Then maybe someday I'd be able to be of service. I was still convinced the Four Thoughts employed scare tactics. But so be it. They were a part of the Hinayana level of the teachings, the narrow way, the blinders on the horse, meant to serve as a container. I'd worked for years to be in this retreat. I didn't need to continue to chafe against the container. And even if I did, I could be friendly with the chafing. Besides, in less than a week we'd begin Ngöndro and prostrations. As demanding as they would be, I knew how to slide onto the floor and then stand up again. That was something I could do.

Chapter Eighteen

PROSTRATIONS AGAIN

After thousands of prostrations, the light thunk of my knees hitting the high-density foam was followed by the swoosh of the beige carpet squares under my hands as they slid down my prostration board. I flattened my body face down, then pushed myself back up to standing. The amber and navy paisley curtain I'd hung across my open doorway gently wafted in the warm breeze. A patch of late summer sun sneaked past the branches of the trees outside my window, bouncing off the walls onto my shiny board.

Anticipating how physically grueling this round of prostrations would be, I'd brought a variety of supplies—tins of tiger balm, tubes of arnica gel, spare pieces of high-density foam, plus a full tub of paste wax to keep my prostration board slick. It had been four years since I completed my first set of prostrations. And I hadn't continued working on that second set as Lama had suggested. I never was much of an athlete and was now almost forty years old—past my prime for this. Lama Norlha was a hardy young monk in Tibet when he completed two three-year retreats before he was twenty-one.

Still, I encouraged myself. I'd finished one set of prostrations. And Trinley successfully completed her three-year retreat, as had other Westerners, some older than me. A few, like Tsupa, more than once. My biggest concern was that my knees might hinder completing the required 111,111.

I pictured the other nuns in their rooms also kneeling and sliding, with more speed, more stamina and more one-pointed concentration. My first round of prostrations had taken slightly more than six months. But in retreat, our assignment was to accumulate 2,500 prostrations each day so we could finish the 111,111 in less than six weeks. Yet, as hard as I pushed, I'd only been able to do about 2,000 per day. But I was here. In retreat. When I noticed my mind meandering or worrying, I took a deep breath, with the reassurance that after completing prostrations we'd move on to the other three practices of Ngöndro. And then we'd be introduced to the practices leading to enlightenment.

Four years earlier, when Trinley and the other retreatants were performing their retreat prostrations, Lama Norlha, seated at the head of the dining table, stretched his arms toward the ceiling before resting his hands on top of his shaved head. "Retreatants working hard, doing prostrations. Needing extra food. I'm telling cooks to make meat soup for dinner. Also putting out cheese and meat for snacks." A few days later, Lama smiled with the pride of a new father, "Tsupa so strong, so much focus. She's finishing prostrations first. Before anyone in men's retreat."

Now we were the recipients of those extra provisions. During our break time after lunch, I snuggled in the corner of my box, imagining Palmo as the victor of our retreat's prostration race. But I didn't need to win–just finish. I visualized myself as the steady turtle in the parable of the tortoise and the hare I read so many times in my youth. *I only have to keep going. I'm practicing for the benefit of all sentient beings.* I penciled cheerleading platitudes in my spiral notebook: *Just do your best. More than that isn't possible anyway. It doesn't matter what anyone else is doing. You'll find your way.*

For ten hours each day, I focused on one prostration at a time, performing this Tibetan version of extreme fitness push-ups, while at night attempting, not very successfully, to sleep sitting up in my meditation box. As the days of intensity accumulated, I knew I was falling behind, maybe so far behind I'd still be working on the last segments of Ngöndro when Lama introduced the new practices. But whoever finished first, I knew Lama wouldn't be around to make an announcement. Shortly after we started this round of prostrations, he traveled to Tibet again. He assured us he wouldn't stay too long, that he'd be back before we completed Ngöndro.

A week after we began our prostrations, I began to feel nauseous, particularly first thing in the morning. Maybe it was a lack of sleep, maybe the physical exertion, or maybe I just couldn't stomach all the effort. Whatever the reason, whenever I ate or even sipped water, I felt queasy. Our breakfast each morning alternated between hot-cooked rolled oats and whole-grain millet. My tender stomach could more easily manage the mushy oatmeal rather than the coarser millet, so I penned a note to our cook and left it for her in the dining room, "Please will you make a small pot of oatmeal for me on the days you're preparing millet. My stomach is giving me trouble and I'm having a hard time with the millet."

That evening, when I returned from chanting, I found a box of packets of instant oatmeal at the door to my room. The next morning, I tore open the little brown packet of instant oatmeal and poured it into my bowl, adding steaming water from my Farberware pot. As I stirred the soggy, soupy little flakes, I wished for fully cooked and simmered cereal to soothe my stomach. Internally steaming, I attempted to talk myself out of my irritation.

Why am I so selfish? Our cook can't take extra time to make something special just for me; she's also trying to complete her prostrations.... Sure, but it's only one extra pot.... Yes, but then she'd have to clean that extra pot. Where's my compassion for her? Why can't I just be satisfied with the millet? Or the instant oatmeal? Why am I so wimpy? But is it wrong to want to take care of my body?

My spinning thoughts would not resolve. Even though I tried

to open, to surrender, to observe this disturbance as simply another arising of my state of consciousness, I repeatedly dissolved into tears of exhausted frustration.

After weeks of prostrating for ten hours each day, the break time after lunch became much more precious. Resting in my box, I leaned my head against the wall, drifting into sleep. Then, bang! The screen door leading to the backyard–to the outhouse and clothesline–closed with a tight metal spring. Unless the person exiting took a moment to hold the door, it would slam, the blow reverberating through the wall next to my box.

I carefully printed a note on a small square of paper and taped it to the screen door, "Please hold the door as it closes. Thank you, Paldrom."

But the slamming continued.

Each time I was startled awake, I glanced out my window and saw the culprit rushing down the back stairs. My stomach would tighten with an urge to press my face against my window screen and scream, "What's wrong with you?" I mentally chastised my retreat-mate as being unconscious and selfish. Then I attempted to wrestle my thoughts into compassion.

She must be so tired, so focused on completing her prostrations (so she can ultimately achieve enlightenment for the benefit of all beings) that she can't be aware of something as mundane as a slamming door. But my mind would whisper: *Is completing the practices really more important than caring for each other?*

As I continued to accumulate my prostrations, the nausea drifted in and out. The increased width of the folds in my shamthap showed that my body was shrinking. I struggled to sleep upright in my box at night. As much as I was determined to remain vertical, as the heaviness of exhaustion pressed on every cell, I sank to the bottom of my box in defeat, curled on my side in a fetal position.

I was sure everyone else was navigating this challenge better than I was. After all, I was the only one bursting into tears, the only one falling asleep while we chanted in the shrine room, my head bobbing, then my chin hitting my chest. I pondered the words I'd written on a three-by-five white index card, translated from one of the prayers we repeated in Tibetan several times each day: "Whatever bad conditions arise, may I come to be able to carry them as companions on the path of developing a mind that strives toward awakening and compassion for the benefit of all sentient beings."

Each morning, I returned to my prostration board. Here emotion was immaterial. Tears or no tears, exhaustion or bursts of energy didn't penetrate the simple unending motion of kneeling, sliding, pushing, standing, all while chanting the prostration prayer. The repetition combined with my focus on the visualization began to dissolve my ordinary perception of time. Prostrations didn't require logic, understanding, or agreement. No need for thought. I could simply melt into the one-pointed simplicity of the physicality of the practice. In the movement there was no doubt, no ambiguity, no comparison, no contradiction.

Day after day after day, I returned my attention to simply completing the prostrations. My body knew exactly what to do. In my mind's eye, I conjured the complex visualization, focusing on one element at a time. I imagined the refuge tree rising from the ground in front of me, filled with deities and their retinues. In the center of the branches, my beloved teacher, Kalu Rinpoche, appeared as the sapphire-blue primordial Buddha, surrounded by all the past teachers of the lineage, including the sixteen Karmapas with their black-hat crowns. On a branch to the left, the Buddhas of the ten directions and the three times. On a branch to the right, Peaceful Chenrezig, white with four arms. Floating on a branch directly in front of me, wrathful Khorlo Demchok in a ring of fire with his four faces and twelve arms, surrounded by his retinue of six deities. On a branch on the back of the tree, books holding the Dharma teachings. I visualized my mother and father standing directly to my right and left, surrounded by my relatives, friends, and acquaintances. Behind me, all beings. Everyone prostrating.

Over, and over, and over again, flat on the ground then back to standing, imagining the scene. I could imagine only one segment of the visualization at a time, and couldn't hold the details in my awareness, but I could rest in the safe harbor, the sanctuary, the shelter of Kalu Rinpoche's quiet grace. And I could repeat the prostration prayer, the syllables washing through my mind.

One late afternoon, after completing thousands of prostrations, I silently whispered the prostration prayer while wearily placing my hands into the indented handprint of my carpet squares. I slid face down onto my prostration board and pushed myself back to a standing position. Then, for just a moment, I paused and stared at my white wall as I visualized the refuge tree and its surrounding retinue of deities. In the waning of the afternoon light, in that moment of pausing, the entire visualization suddenly appeared as a peaceful, silent, brilliant white glow—a radiance not imagined, not visualized, but actually present. Luminous white light penetrated the room, penetrated me. Maybe it was the stillness of the afternoon sunlight, or the silence of the warm breeze, or maybe the lack of sleep and nutrition created an overload, a short circuit, in my body and brain.

I sat down on my prostration board. I wasn't separate from this silent wholeness. I couldn't be. Nothing was needed. Nothing was missing. Nothing to do. Nowhere to go. I was simply home. In those few ordinary extraordinary moments of clarity, I knew that all, every appearance, was simply an out-picturing of this embracing, silent, clear expansiveness.

After a perilous journey down the yellow brick road in Oz, Dorothy saw Toto yank on a curtain and reveal the true identity of the "great and powerful" wizard. That revelation changed her view of reality forever. Watery instant oatmeal, a jarring screen door, exhaustion, comparing, questioning, doubting, even my delicate emotionality–had all led directly to this penetrating moment of grace, to this yanking of the curtain. And even though I'd try, I couldn't unsee what had been revealed.

Chapter Nineteen

THE RIGHTNESS OF WRONG

I was not in my box. Instead, I was stretched out flat on the cool plywood floor, staring at the moonlit ceiling and trying to obliterate the certainty that I could not–must not–remain in this retreat. I recalled each logical, good, pure, even holy, reason for being here. But nothing could touch the clawing pull to go. We were supposed to be protected, locked away from the world behind the stockade fence, yet I could not stop the percolating thoughts that threatened to end my retreat.

Every question, doubt, and concern descended in a wild, mad dance, shrieking that I needed to leave. I reminded myself that these snarling impulses were simply demons and prayed they depart. But they did not. They were in full possession of every thought. Each time I pushed them away, they crept back, mingling in the sandalwood incense smoke snaking toward the ceiling like a genie escaping from an ageless decanter.

Not a sliver remained of the inner clarity, the home I'd experienced on my prostration board only two weeks earlier. Bathed in stillness, I'd crawled into the containing shelter of my box and leaned my head against the wall under my window, telling myself I'd return to prostrations in the next practice session. I just needed a brief respite.

Yet after dinner, after placing my prostration board on the floor, as my knees dropped to the yellowing piece of foam, as my hands found the beige carpeting scraps and slid down the board, as I again attempted to visualize the refuge tree and its multiple inhabitants, the entire process seemed incongruously complicated. Silence beckoned, with its welcoming simplicity. Prostrations could wait. I poured my body back into my box, slumped against the wall, and closed my eyes. With each deep breath, the quiet penetrated and expanded my cells.

The following morning, afternoon, and evening, and for several more days, I attempted prostrations, but couldn't find the motivation to resume. Resting in my box, I knew I was falling further and further behind. I repeatedly resolved to end my prostration intermission, to begin again in the next, then the next, then the next practice session.

Before Lama left for Tibet, he advised that, although not optimal, we could combine performing prostrations with the second segment of Ngöndro. So, on the fifth morning of my lost motivation, I decided to begin accumulating the required 111,111 Dorje Sempa mantra repetitions while filling myself with purifying white light. I soothed myself with the promise I'd return to prostrations in a couple of days. But even Dorje Sempa's relatively simple visualization seemed complicated, forced, artificial.

Day after day, I watched as shadows crept across my white walls. *Why can't I find a way to do the practices? Do I even want to? Will repeating a required number of mantras, then moving on to another visualization practice, to another set of mantra repetitions, really lead to enlightenment?*

These misgivings about the practices reopened the cracks of doubt that had surfaced during my first weeks contemplating the Four Thoughts–thoughts that were meant to be a support in turning my mind to the dharma, but instead became such a challenge. I needed to once again find a way to adjust my thinking. Although these newest considerations beckoned with inherent clarity, they were certainly not welcome. *I worked for five years to be in this retreat so I could learn the practices leading to enlightenment. I have to find a way to do them.*

Seeking solace, attempting to surrender, I focused on my shrine–on my picture of Kalu Rinpoche–and melted into the warmth of devotion. *My participation in this retreat was blessed by Rinpoche. I received the empowerments for the practices taught in this retreat from him ... twice. Doesn't that mean I have a commitment to him to learn them?*

I reminded myself that these rituals had been handed down over the centuries, honed by awakened masters to lift the veil of illusory, samsaric existence by creating alternative realities, by embodying enlightened qualities, by transforming oneself in order to ultimately become capable of benefiting others. Three years was the prescribed length of time to first learn, and then solidify the practice of these techniques. Then, after completing the retreat, I'd continue repeating these practices every day for the rest of my life. But how could I do that when I couldn't even find a way to complete this set of prostrations, only the first of the preliminary practices? *I have to start practicing again. Otherwise, I'll never be enlightened. I'll never truly be of service.*

I visualized a transformed version of myself after three years in retreat. *Who will I be? Will I become like Tsupa?... I'm not sure I want that.* Lama's star student seemed unhappy, even angry. *Or like our cook?* Her attention was focused on completing repetitions, just like Trinley. *Will I too become absorbed with racking up a set amount of practice each day, on repeating mantras? What about friendly kindness, ordinary compassion, care for each other?*

I began to entertain alternatives to remaining in retreat. *Maybe I can focus on service, on benefiting others somehow. Maybe I could use the funds I've saved to train in some kind of therapeutic healing. Then at least I could help alleviate physical suffering.*

I wrote a letter to the nun who was Lama Norlha's head administrator and shared my plan for service, hoping she'd appreciate my bodhisattva intention. I fantasized she'd recognize the merits of my plan—and perhaps even relay her understanding of my reasoning to Lama when he returned.

Days passed as I waited for her reply. Each morning and afternoon I joined my retreat-mates as we silently filed up the stairs for puja. We ate lunch without speaking, seated on the floor around the dining room table. I avoided direct eye contact, careful to not somehow reveal what I was doing—or not doing—in my room during our practice sessions.

When a small white envelope from Lama's administrator finally arrived, I climbed into my box, carefully unsealed the flap, and removed two pages of blue-lined notebook paper filled with her precisely penned words. I scanned each line searching for a hint of approval. But she only pointed to the shortsightedness of my reasoning and the folly of abandoning the incalculable (and rare) benefits of learning the practices offered in retreat.

I stared out my window, noting the varieties of greens of the trees, the browns in the dirt, the graying fence, the burgundy outhouse, trying to reclaim the motivation to participate, to perform prostrations once again, or to repeat Dorje Sempa's mantra. Instead, I penciled my reservations in one of my little notebooks:

- How do I know this desire to leave isn't just my resistance to discipline?
- How do I know I'm not just copping out and refusing to exit samsara when I have the chance?
- Is being in this retreat the only way to reach enlightenment?

My dreams were filled with images pointing to the need to leave. I dreamt my box was filled with pus and excrement or was inhabited by a rat. I dreamt of a young wandering woman who was poking her eye out with a stick. I dreamt of meeting a healer who directly instructed, "You need to leave retreat." Yet, even with the clarity of these dream images, I couldn't override my desperate clinging to the promised reward of learning the practices, of completing a three-year retreat.

Long past midnight, when I was meant to be contained and meditatively sleeping in my box–certainly not allowed to leave my room–I'd slipped silently out the back screen door and wrapped my arms around the trunk of a stars-reaching tree, begging for relief, for a restoration of my broken, lost capacity.

Returning to my room, I squirmed in my box, incapable of sleep, unable to find a comfortable way to arrange my body. Crawling out of my box, I smoothed my sleeping bag onto the floor, then stretched out on top of it.

Staring at the ceiling, I experimented with releasing each piece of my desire to leave, attempting to reclaim the core of my resolve to stay. Like shedding layers of clothing, then skin, bone, blood, and breath, I let go bit by bit until there was nothing, no one, left to rise from the floor and perform the practices. But as soon as even a piece of a me–of a someone–returned, even that tiniest bit of me held the impossible, unacceptable certainty that it was time to go.

All I could hear was the sound of my breathing, the slight pop of a candle on my altar, the ash from the smoky cedar and sandalwood incense hitting the rice that held the stick. Drowning in the knowledge that I had to leave, gasping for a resolve to stay, dreading utter failure, with the tiniest exhale, there was only one thing left to do. The one single thing I'd avoided for the past five years since I first imagined participating in a three-year retreat. The one wrong thing I never imagined could be so right. I gave up.

Chapter Twenty

NOT MY MEDICINE

We were waiting for Lama in the central foyer, standing in front of the doors to our rooms. I stared at the floor. Now he was back. He knew. He'd been told I was leaving. As I shifted my gaze from the burgundy floor to the wood stove's chimney pipe, I could hear myself breathing. *What will Lama say? What will he do? Will I be escorted off the grounds under the cover of darkness? Be strong. You can do this.*

Unable to predict the consequences of my decision, I could only hold tight to my certainty. More than that was impossible. A month earlier, I'd written again to the center's administrator, thanking her for her kind advice and asking that she inform Lama of my plans to leave the retreat when he returned. Even though I now seriously doubted he'd bless my decision, out of respect I delayed my departure until I could face him directly. Also, I wanted him to temporarily open the seal of protection we'd been told was holding us, guarding us within the fences of the retreat. I didn't want to risk disturbing any invisible protector beings–the dakas, dakinis, wisdom beings, and any nature spirits or local deities. I'd seen enough unexplainable phenomena to warrant caution.

The entry vestibule's inner door creaked open and clicked closed, followed by a few moments of silence. Lama had arrived and was now crossing the dirt yard. Then his footsteps resounded on the stairs, like prayer flags snapping in a strong wind. The screen door opened and closed, and he appeared, his brown slip-on loafers pointing diagonally toward the corners of the room. Glancing to his left, he smiled at our cook. She dipped her head slightly, smiling back, "Hi, Lama. So good to see you."

He continued looking around the room, focusing his attention on each of us, one at a time. When his gaze found me, he stopped, stared directly, blinked, then looked again. Was he seeing through me? Inside me? Was he disgusted? What did he perceive?

He narrowed his eyes. "Paldrom leaving retreat."

I dared not breathe. *Well, there it is. Now everyone knows.* The only other person in the retreat who knew about my plan to leave was Chodrin.

While waiting for Lama's return, I'd volunteered to serve as one of the two chöpons during our puja chanting sessions, filling and emptying the water bowls and polishing one set of the bowls each day. I imagined this was a small way to be of service, to embody bodhisattva qualities. Even though I'd careened off the tracks, at least I could help those who were still on this path to enlightenment.

One late afternoon, Chodrin and I were downstairs in the central foyer each polishing a set of offering bowls. Yellow rubber gloves protected our hands, red cotton scarves covered our noses and mouths. She fidgeted as she worked, like someone who'd consumed too much coffee. As she slathered some gray cleaning goo into a copper bowl, she poked me with her elbow. "Hey, did you finish your prostrations yet?"

We were only allowed to converse with each other during our after-lunch break time, and then only to briefly share routine information more easily spoken than written. Evidently, she wasn't committed to following this rule.

She whispered, but so quickly and with such intensity, I was concerned someone might hear. I looked around, assuring myself that everyone else was upstairs in the lhakhang chanting.

Shaking my head in a gesture of no, I widened my eyes, then tilted my head slightly. *Really? She wants me to talk with her? Maybe I should. Maybe she's having a hard time with all this silence and isolation.*

She nudged me again, her gloved hands holding a bowl in one hand, a rag in the other. "I finished mine last week. I think Palmo finished first. You're probably not even close."

Unseen behind my scarf, I smiled at her conclusion, at her familiar prodding. She was right. Palmo probably did finish first. And I wasn't close to finishing. I nodded silently.

She tried again, "How many prostrations do you have left?"

I stared at her, raising my eyebrows, hoping she'd realize I didn't want to talk.

"How many?" She waited for a few moments for my response. When I continued looking at her, blinking without speaking, she continued, "No one can hear us."

She wasn't going to give up. I placed the copper bowl I was cleaning onto the rag in my lap, then pulled on the scarf covering my mouth and nose, leaving it hanging around my neck. "I stopped doing prostrations. I'm leaving retreat as soon as Lama gets back."

She laughed, "Yeah, right."

Tugging on the end of one of the yellow gloves at my wrist to snug my fingertips more securely, I smiled. "Watch me."

I pulled the scarf back onto my mouth and nose and picked up the bowl, continuing to smooth away the tarnish. Wide-eyed, she'd stared at me for a few moments, then returned her gaze to the bowl she'd been cleaning.

Now Chodrin wasn't the only one who knew I was leaving. Lama announced it to everyone. It was official. No turning back. Before I had even a moment to dread what he might say next, he continued. "When Paldrom decides to come back in retreat, we let her."

I quietly gulped some air, determined to not leak any emotion. *But what was I feeling? I knew I wasn't going to return, didn't I? Was this a trick?* I scrambled for an answer. At least I wasn't going to be banished. Staring at the floor, I took another deep breath. *This is going to work out.*

After Lama finished looking around the circle, he announced he was tired and needed to rest, but assured us he'd return after breakfast the next day to present teachings. I wondered what his lesson might be since it wasn't yet time to learn a new practice. Everyone was still working on completing their retreat set of the four Ngöndro practices. I'd be gone before any of the advanced teachings were introduced.

The next morning after breakfast, I climbed the stairs to the lhakhang, the wood cool beneath my bare feet. Lama was waiting for us, seated on a cushion against the wall under the windows. As we entered, we silently performed the three customary partial prostrations, then settled onto our cushions.

Lama began with an admonition to not waste the rare opportunity of being born into a human realm. I looked straight ahead, focusing on the shrine and the shiny bowls full of still water. The uncontrived melody of songbirds drifted in through the open windows.

Here we go again. The scare tactics. I've heard this all before. It won't change my mind.

Overnight, I'd consolidated my justification for not returning to retreat. I was going to use my saved funds to learn some alternative healing modality.

Chodrin and a few of the other nuns glanced in my direction. *Everyone now believes I'm a failure. Maybe I am. Maybe I've lost my mind ... but I can't let my uncertainty show.*

Lama continued, repeating the teachings on the precious human existence and the blessing of being a human who encounters the wisdom of the Buddha. Next he progressed to an explanation of the rarest of all opportunities–the chance to participate in a three-year retreat.

Closing my eyes, I leaned against the wall. My toes started to twitch. *I want to believe what Lama's saying. I understand the importance of trusting my teacher. Still, I can't stay.*

He continued by describing the folly of returning empty-handed from a land of wish-fulfilling gems. Then he paused, leaning forward slightly, resting his forearms on a pecha bench. "Must never leave retreat. Must only think, stay in retreat. No run. If leaving retreat, no good ever coming in this life. Rest of life, no good."

I'd never heard this warning before. I kept my eyes closed. I didn't want to see anyone's reaction. *Nothing in my life will ever be good again? Then how can I go? Maybe I'm doomed. But I can't stay. I cannot stay.*

Since surrendering on my plywood floor, I hadn't cried once. But now tears began to stream down my face. My breath started to shake, on the verge of dissolving into sobs. *Don't let anyone see. Listen to the birds.* But their song was now as absent as my capacity to contain this emotion.

Rising as silently as possible, head bowed to the floor, I slipped out, descended the stairs to my room, and curled up in the corner of my box, blubbering in weepy confusion. *This is too much. Nothing will ever be good again? I don't think I'm strong enough to leave. But I have to go.*

Unable to reason my way out of this dilemma, I distracted myself from the uncontrollable cavorting of uncertainty and dread by focusing on the in-and-out movement of my breath. I don't know how long I waited in that suspended state of frozen bewilderment, but long enough for Lama to complete his teaching session. Then, from the other side of the curtain hanging in my doorway, I heard someone quietly calling my name. "Paldrom. Paldrom. Lama wants to talk to you."

When I pushed my curtain aside, I saw Lama sitting cross-legged on the floor in front of the wood stove. He motioned, "You sit. Everyone still upstairs. Meditating."

Staring at Lama's emotionless face, I lowered myself onto the hard floor in front of him. Before he could say a word, I blurted, "Lama, I don't know what to do. I have to leave. I want to study some kind of healing so I can help people. Then I can make money to support the people here who want to do retreat."

"No want your money made from sin."

"Sin?" I couldn't imagine how my plan would create sin, but it was clear he wasn't going to approve.

"But Lama, I can't stay. I just can't. But now I can't go either. Nothing in my life will ever be good again."

Lama's eyes softened and he smiled. "That not your medicine. No think that."

Not my medicine? Did he just remove his curse? He did. But then why did he say it?

He stretched his arms toward the ceiling, piling his hands on top of his head. "Next Tuesday very auspicious day. Good day for you leaving retreat house. You stay in new cabin we build for short retreats. Stay there until ready to come back here. Now go. Others want some talking with me."

I returned to my room, to my box. *Lama didn't demand that I stay. So why did he speak so provocatively about leaving?* His curse and the rescinding of it smacked against the stillness of my room. As I sat in that unsettled quiet, ripples of memory began to surface, softening my tangle of confusion and doubt.

I thought of Lama's deception about Chodrin and Palmo's preparations to travel to India. And I remembered how he questioned

Kalu Rinpoche's instruction regarding samaya with the Vajra Regent. Then I remembered a story Lama had shared years earlier. When he was in the Chinese prison camp, he managed to keep his mala from being confiscated. I remembered how he laughed as he described strategically looking for the guard with the kindest face and offering his mala in a gesture of utter (although feigned) respect and surrender. The guard declined the offering.

Lama certainly knows how to get what he wants. He'll say or do anything he thinks will be beneficial. He wants to be sure no one else follows my lead. I shook my head as I reflected on his wily tactics—and at the intensity of my reaction, the bungee-jump extremes of my emotional response.

That night I watched the night sky from my window, listening to the rustling leaves. In the quiet of my room, in the expanse of the stars, I recalled the Buddha's teaching to rely on the source of one's own experience—belief or faith or blind devotion not required. I knew again and with an even deeper certainty that I would leave, that I could trust myself—regardless of what Lama Norlha had said or might say. Even though this might be the biggest mistake of my life, it was a trustworthy mistake, arising from a still clarity closer than any thought or reasoning.

Chapter Twenty-one
FORTY

During the afternoon practice session—while my retreat-mates were securely ensconced in their rooms—Tsupa, as she had three and a half months earlier, helped load my belongings into the back of the center's pickup truck. We took a short ride down the hill to a newly constructed one-room cabin. The sweet scent of fresh lumber greeted me when I opened the door. Lingering in the doorway, I noted that this room looked much like the room I'd just abandoned—flat white walls and a glossy burgundy plywood floor. But no box. And it had a bed—a twin-sized mattress resting on a plywood platform with legs constructed from unpainted two-by-fours.

This box-lessness was a clear indication I'd left the three-year retreat. Even though Lama Norlha seemed to believe this little cabin would be my retreat halfway house, a place to stay until I came to my senses, I knew I wouldn't return. And that I'd never again attempt sleeping in a meditation box. However, I soon discovered my attempts to sleep sitting up had birthed a new capacity. I could now, especially when weary, simply close my eyes while seated and enjoy a short nap, often without my chin bobbing toward my chest.

After Tsupa helped carry my metal trunk filled with supplies into this new room, I plopped down on the bed. She paused in the doorway. "Lama wanted me to let you know someone can bring your dinner to you."

Smiling half-heartedly, I nodded. "Thanks."

Then she was gone. I was completely alone. Surprisingly, more alone than I'd been in my retreat room. I had no practice obligations to ignore and, at least for now, no required attendance at puja, no chores, no money to earn. But rather than experiencing expansive freedom, I felt adrift, like a birthday balloon floating away from the grasp of its young owner.

Smoothing my sleeping bag onto the bed, I stretched out on its cool silkiness, sighed deeply, closed my eyes, then melted into the embracing support of the mattress. *So now what? Lama must imagine I'm so embarrassed that I won't want to face anyone—that I'll want to hide in this little cabin until I decide to go back into retreat. How long does he think I'll camp out in here?*

All I could do was close my eyes and watch my breath. No one was going to appear to provide consolation or support. I imagined facing Dechi and Drupten, the other monks and nuns, and any visiting guests. *Everyone is going to think my leaving is a shameful disappointment, that I've failed. And I have. I couldn't complete the retreat. I barely got started.*

The splinters of inadequacy embedded in my decision to leave the retreat wouldn't fully dissolve for many years. But for now, on this cushy mattress, I watched this parade of judgment, these flares of shame, with a curiously unattached spaciousness. As the daylight waned, I opened my eyes and stared at the ceiling. *Either today, tomorrow, next week, or next month, I'm going to have to bear all the judging eyes.*

As a kid, I experienced how much easier it was to jump right into the cold swimming pool rather than endure the extended pricking of cold needles from wading in inch by inch. I smiled as "get back on the horse" echoed in my thoughts. Although I was never thrown from a horse, I pictured myself sprawled in the dirt, stunned, afraid. The wisdom of avoiding delay floated into clarity like a response appearing on a Magic 8 Ball: GO NOW. *I can't wait to face the world outside this room. I might lose my resolve.*

When the gong rang as a summons to puja, I stood up, wrapped my zen around my body flipping one end over my left shoulder, picked up my pechas, then headed out across the parking lot striding with all the determination I could muster. After all, I was still a nun. And I could still chant, even if I would not, could not, complete retreat.

Entering the lhakhang with eyes down, I performed three prostrations and took a spot in the middle of the nun's row. I placed my pechas on the shiny ruby-red bench, opened them to the section of our evening chanting, then closed my eyes in meditation until Lama Norlha began. As we chanted, I focused on the familiar drone of Lama's voice, of our voices, the shrill of the horns, the clanging of the cymbals, the steady, steady beat of the drum. Afterwards, in the dining room, avoiding conversation, I filled my bowl with yogurt topped with a big spoonful of strawberry jam, smiling at anyone who caught my eyes, determined to maintain my I-know-what-I'm-doing demeanor. Then, slipping out the back door with my bowl of yogurt, I returned to my new room.

That night in bed, turning onto my side, I pulled my knees close to my chest. *I can't stay here if I'm going to study healing work. But I can still be a nun—just a nun out in the world.*

Within a week, I found a room to rent in the home of a married couple, chiropractors whose offices I'd cleaned to earn retreat funds. Their large cottage, surrounded by acres of woods with a bubbling creek, was about an hour's drive from the monastery. This was my true retreat halfway house. Enveloped in the silence of these surroundings, held in the grace of the generous support of my chiropractic friends, I began to reacclimate to life in the world.

The months of minimal external stimulation in retreat had amplified my sensitivity to sensory input. I was nakedly fragile, less naturally armored. The first time I visited a fast-food chain restaurant, the moist heat of the french fries smelled like ambrosia, the colors and sounds were stunningly vibrant, as if magic dust had been sprinkled on the glistening white, red, and yellow plastic. Sometimes I experienced puzzling waves of emotion–then realized I was registering emotional vibrations from someone in my immediate vicinity. My sense of time was fluid, amorphous. While mashing potatoes for Thanksgiving dinner, I timelessly melted into the swirling creamy contents of a green glass bowl.

One of my first steps into life outside the monastery was finding employment as a clerk in a small, natural foods deli where I ladled healthy soups, salads, and desserts into plastic containers, rang sales into a clanking cash register, dispensed change, scrubbed pots and pans, and polished the glass on the display case. On my days off, I took long walks on dirt country roads. In the evenings, I often joined my hosts in their living room, stretching out on a braided rug in front of the fireplace, listening as one of them read a chapter aloud from books unlike anything I'd experienced for years–like Douglas Adams's *The Hitchhiker's Guide to the Galaxy*.

For hours I stared out my bedroom window, absorbed in the daytime and nighttime sky. In one of my spiral-bound notebooks, I started to pen a new myth, a fairytale representing this latest configuration of the kaleidoscopic manifestation of my life. And I began looking for a training program in some healing modality. In these days before Google, I scanned advertisements sprinkled in the back pages of yoga and meditation magazines, then sent for brochures from massage therapy training programs in California, Arizona, and New Mexico.

As weeks, then months passed, my need and desire to maintain the rigidity of my vows gradually dissipated. I stopped wearing my robes. Although my vows had been a support, a way to belong, I was ready to leave their sheltering structure. Observing the sweetness of my married hosts' relationship, I wondered if I too might someday find a lover, a husband. I didn't fantasize reuniting with Dan, but imagined sharing my life with a partner, an equal.

Monastic vows are relinquished by giving them back to the teacher who bestowed them. But Kalu Rinpoche had died. His reincarnation had recently been recognized but was only a year old ... and was living in India. If I was going to return my vows, Lama Norlha was my only viable option. So, five months after leaving the monastery I called and arranged a meeting.

On a blazing, sunny May afternoon, I returned to the monastery. No one came to greet me as I entered the main house carrying my foot-high pile of robes. After kicking off my shoes, I climbed the stairs, peeked into the lhakhang as I passed it, then quietly padded down the hallway toward Lama's room. I found him in his large anteroom, standing, waiting for me.

I walked toward him smiling and offering the stack of my robes—several saffron yellow shirts with buttons shaped like tiny brass bells, two burgundy woolen shamthaps, a woolen tonga, and two zens. The small cotton packet I'd worn next to my body for years rested on the top of the pile. It held the strips of cloth blessed with the essence of the vows bestowed by Kalu Rinpoche in Bodh Gaya. I was returning my clothing so someone else could make use of it, but returning the packet of cloth was representative of relinquishing my vows.

"Lama, I want to return my vows. I can't give them back to Kalu Rinpoche. Will you please take them?"

I'd dreaded this moment, imagining how in accepting the return he'd also rain descriptions of the foolishness of my rejection of a multitude of sacred and rare opportunities. With not a trace of reaction, he reached out and took the pile of clothing from my arms, placing it on a nearby small table. Then he picked up the cotton packet from the top of the pile. Squinting, he held it out to me. "I no keep. No join you in this sin."

He wasn't going to let me return my vows. "Okay," I quietly nodded. I couldn't think of anything else to say, so I accepted the cloth bundle, then backed out of the room.

When I exited the front door, I noticed the ever-present line of battered prayer flags hanging silently between two trees, unmoving in the afternoon stillness. Most of the prayers on the threads of those flags had been released into the air by the wind. Without stopping, I headed back toward my car.

Sunlight sparkled and danced in the gravel of the parking lot. As it crunched under my feet, I heard someone calling my name, so I stopped and turned. Dechi had rushed out the front door toward me waving a foot-and-a-half long red piece of thick string, a protection cord to wear like a necklace. She was slightly out of breath when she reached me.

"Here," she thrust the cord in my direction. "Lama told us at lunch that you were coming by, and that you were possessed by demons. This will protect you."

I felt a twinge of fear. Maybe it was true. I stared at the ground. The air was so still, so bright, so rarefied, that every rock in the driveway glistened. *Not my medicine.*

I smiled and accepted her offering, "Thanks. I'm okay. Really."

Her shoulders dropped as she turned to head back toward the main house.

In my car, I placed the protection cord and the cloth packet that Lama had rejected onto the passenger seat, then focused on the homes dotting the bank across the Hudson River. They appeared exactly as they had six years earlier when I decided to stay, when I first imagined I might someday be able to participate in a three-year retreat. The storyline of my life had certainly departed from that plan.

Aware of a pressure in my chest—no tears, just weight—I shook my head in a vigorous back-and-forth motion, like a dog shaking off water after a swim. With this gesture, the heaviness burst. The greedy, fearful grasping for something I thought I'd discover in the three-year retreat dissolved into timeless no-thought. I started my car's engine, placed my hands on the steering wheel, and slowly drove away from the monastery along the long, bumpy driveway. My search for enlightenment had not ended, but something had cracked open. And like Humpty-Dumpty after his tumble from a wall, I could not put myself back together again.

A week later, on my fortieth birthday, at dusk, I stood with my hosts, my friends, encircling a small campfire they had built for the occasion. As the smoky warmth from the burning logs warmed our toes, I shared the fairy tale I had just written, *Dragon Flight*. When I finished reading, we stood in silence, sipping on green-bottled imported beer and munching on the hot dogs we'd roasted. Then as the sun dipped below the horizon, I threw the strips of cloth holding my vows into the fire, one at a time. Each burst into flame before disappearing.

Dragon Flight

> The group of young dragons trudged wearily through the snow, led by their elder, Mighty Norbu. "Oh-om," they chanted as they walked. The sounds of their voices echoed off the mountains that encircled this huge plateau. Sunlight glistened on their amethyst skin. In the late afternoon light, their orange spikes resembled the fire they could breathe.
>
> They walked and chanted in this way until the sun began to set. The full moon glowed in the eastern sky. Mighty Norbu led the young dragons into an enormous cave–their sacred gathering hall.
>
> Each young dragon ceremoniously presented

a log the length of his span– "from nose to tail tip" according to ancient custom. Mighty Norbu lit the logs with his powerful breath of fire.

While the dragons sat motionless around this full-moon fire, the evening's lessons began. "Oh-om," they chanted together before Mighty Norbu spoke.

"A dragon's job in this world is to appear fierce. Always remember this. A dragon's fierce appearance ensures his survival and the survival of all dragons. Our appearance is our life, and our life is maintaining the standard of ferocity."

Dorje's mind shifted uncomfortably. He dared not move. His thoughts drifted to visions of laughing and flying ... of circling in the air, turning patches of snow into huge ponds with a burst of fire shot to earth with his forceful breath. He almost let a smile creep across his face. But Mighty Norbu's words quickly brought his wandering mind back into the cave.

"Remember our dragon vows. They bind and preserve us. Living here at the top of the world, hidden in this valley surrounded by snow peaks, our kind remains only because of our discipline. To maintain this discipline, we must hold tight to our first vow of always retaining a fierce expression.

"Secondly, fire must only come from the mouths of the senior dragons. And that only in ceremony. Fire is a precious substance that has been misunderstood by those who are not our kind."

He instructed them, as so many times before, "This is the second vow. Do not breathe fire. If your mind thinks of fire breathing, remind yourself of the danger."

Mighty Norbu paused sternly. "Always remember: flying is the most dangerous thing a dragon can do. To maintain our safety, hidden here in the mountains, we all must remain on the ground. Flying puts us all at risk. Walking and chanting binds us to mother earth and father sound. For this reason, your third vow is to remain firmly on the ground at all times. Now, let us chant the vows together."

Led by Mighty Norbu, the young dragons repeated the dragon vows in their ancient tongue. Dorje didn't fully understand all the words, only pieces of the ancient language, but he certainly understood the meaning of what he chanted.

His longings for flight, and to joyfully breathe fire, made him squirm as he chanted with the rest of the group. But soon enough he and his dragon brothers continued repeating the ancient syllables over and over and over, first slowly, then faster and faster, until their minds were abuzz as one.

The moon crept across the sky as they chanted. One by one the young dragons drifted off to sleep until only echoes of their chanting circled the fire.

Dorje was the last to sleep, but in time his head began nodding as well. As his head dropped, he dreamt....

He was flying above the snowbanks of the far-reaching peaks. As he flew, he was laughing and breathing fire that shot up in the air turning a multitude of colors and then showering back down onto the earth. Each place a drop of his fire shower hit turned into a tiny pond. In the center of each of these ponds a flower appeared, each a different color, matching the drop of firelight that had created the pond.

As Dorje looked at each of the flowers more closely, he noticed that in the center of an amethyst-colored flower a tiny amethyst dragon who looked remarkably like him was singing.

> Fly, dear Dorje, fly
> Fly on wings, high in the sky.
> Laugh, dear Dorje, laugh,
> Do not fear, this is your path.

Suddenly, amid dark clouds, Dorje glimpsed Mighty Norbu's frowning face hovering in the sky above.

"Oh, my," Dorje gasped, "the Dragon Vows."

The tiny dragon looked straight into Dorje's eyes. "Do not fear. Long, long ago, dragons were revered. They were known as children of thunder and lightning. They played in the heavens, breathing fire seen as rainbows. Their singing, heard as the whistling wind, echoed throughout the land.

"In time, dragons began to compare the strength and color of their fire, the cleverness of their songs. At first the competition was friendly, but over the ages dragons began to fight dragons. The dragon wars began. In time, these wars threatened to destroy us all. Finally, the fiercest dragons established the Dragon Order. This was necessary.

"These eons of remaining on the ground, of chanting, of listening, of stilling, have begun to tame the fierce dragon mind. But now, dear Dorje, for some dragons, it's time to go. It will not be easy. But know, there will be others. You will find others."

Dorje awoke with a start. He looked around the cave at his sleeping dragon brothers. He straightened his posture and began quietly chanting the dragon vows in the ancient tongue as he had been taught. But mixed with the sound of his chanting, he heard a tiny voice singing:

> Fly, dear Dorje, fly
> Fly on wings, high in the sky.
> Laugh, dear Dorje, laugh,
> Do not fear, this is your path.

Without a sound, without a thought, Dorje arose and walked to the mouth of the cave. Lifting his wings, he laughed and flew toward the snow mountains.

EPILOGUE

More than three decades have passed since my years spent with the Tibetans. Easing into the comfort of my brocaded chair, ever mindful of arthritic knees, I watch as tiny yellow-breasted wrens approach the gurgling water fountain on my deck, dip their beaks, then fly away. They return moments, maybe hours, later. I rest here for moments, maybe hours, at times drifting into sleep. Nestled in this cozy chair, laptop resting on my thighs, memories arise like echoes, shadows forming into words describing the transcendent moments–and the disillusionments.

My story is not a road map. Renouncing life in the world and retreating to a monastery is not necessary, even though it seems *I* needed to attempt to sleep sitting up in a meditation box locked in a tiny room. Yet my immersion in the Tibetan world bestowed blessed glimpses of clarity. Slowly, often imperceptibly, the tendrils of those glimpses continue to grow.

Even though I'd learned to watch the rise and fall of my emotions, I still imagined I could transcend them. I still longed for an escape hatch leading to a heavenly land where my troubles would melt like lemon drops. In challenging moments, I'd sometimes fantasize escape to a simple cloistered life, before reminding myself that I'd already tried it.

Although my decision to leave the monastery was unavoidably clear, I continued to visit an internal ghetto littered with thoughts of failure. After all, I didn't succeed in completing a three-year retreat–something other Westerners, including Trinley and Palmo, were able to do. In fact, Palmo completed two, and Trinley, three.

After leaving the monastery, I spent six months with my chiropractic friends, sheltered in the sanctuary of their cottage in the woods. Then I moved to Santa Fe, New Mexico, to take an eighteen-month course in massage therapy. I earned my massage license, relocated to Boulder, Colorado, and began building my practice.

Shortly after arriving in Boulder, I attended a meeting, a *satsang*, led by a Western woman named Gangaji. Her teacher was Papaji, an Eastern mystic in the Advaita lineage of Ramana Maharshi. In Gangaji's words, I recognized the essence of the "pointing-out" instructions I'd first heard from Kalu Rinpoche soon after arriving at the monastery. With no need for translation, Gangaji's words also elucidated the concepts I first encountered in Khenpo Tsultrim's instruction on the classical Mahamudra text.

I arranged my schedule so I could attend every Gangaji satsang meeting, four or five each week. Then, on Friday afternoons, I volunteered to answer the phones at the offices of her nonprofit organization, the Gangaji Foundation. After only a few months of volunteering I was offered part-time paid employment as the organization's bookkeeping assistant. This seemed ideal–I could earn a bit of steady income while growing my fledgling massage practice. But my part-time role at the Foundation quickly expanded to full-time, with no time left for massage.

The Tibetan visualization practices, imagining the compassion of the deity, then imagining embodying that compassion, had opened pathways of devotion. When Gangaji entered the room at a satsang meeting, every vestige of fearful tension melted into a deep, all-is-right-with-the-world knowing. The first time I had an opportunity to meet with her privately, I finally understood a prostration. After I walked into the room, even though I simply sat down in the chair that was waiting for me, my very being-ness was flat on the floor at her feet.

For the next fourteen years, I worked long days and nights as the Foundation's financial manager. Although unaware of it at the time, I was incubating, shaded by the umbrella of my devotion to Gangaji and her organization's mission of serving "the truth of universal consciousness and the potential for the individual and collective recognition of peace inherent in the core of all being." I'd found a way to be of service, not in the healing arts, but by supporting Gangaji and the mission of her Foundation.

Even though I'd imagined the possibility of a romantic partnership when I left monastic life, ten years later, I concluded that intimate partnership was just not going to be an option for me. But then I started dating another of Gangaji's students, a man who counsels sex addicts. When we decided to marry, I pictured building a relationship like the one Gangaji had with her husband, Eli Jaxon-Bear, also a spiritual teacher. When Eli disclosed a three-year secret affair with a student, I was stunned–I'd worked alongside this student, a young woman, and never suspected. Yet I wasn't as shocked as many others in the community, perhaps because of what I'd learned about Kalu Rinpoche's secret sexual life.

When Rinpoche was seventy years old, his translator, a western nun in her twenties, had also been his sexual consort. Although sworn to secrecy at the time, eighteen years later she authored a book sharing her insights about this confusing and unequal relationship. When I first discovered her writings, I attempted to reconcile how Kalu Rinpoche–the man I'd visualized as a manifestation of pure consciousness, the primordial Buddha, an ultra-evolved human, someone who demonstrated vast qualities of harmlessness, who pacified wild birds, who appeared to be an E.T.–could have been blind to the harm of his secret sexual liaison with his devoted young student.

I rationalized that perhaps he lacked a basic understanding of the emotional power of human connectedness inherent in intimate sexual contact. In Tibet, the highest honor for bright-eyed young boys was to be placed in a monastery and raised by monks. There, they were encouraged to view human connection as a distraction to escaping from the unending suffering of cyclic samsara. I imagined that Kalu Rinpoche might have viewed his relationship with his translator as tantric ritual, like yab-yum deities in sexual embrace. Even though my experiences with Dan had shown how confusing (and painful) this kind of sexual relationship and attachment can be, I'd also directly experienced the transformative force of sexual connection.

With Eli's disclosure, my focus remained on serving Gangaji, maintaining my self-imposed mandate to guard the financial stability and legal integrity of her organization. The challenge of that imperative, combined with the challenge of life with a husband, offered continuing opportunities to surrender as I had on my retreat room floor. Still, my capacity to surrender was spotty. But I was expert at acquiring the skills and knowledge needed to perform the tasks required by my ever-shifting responsibilities in my work at Gangaji's foundation. I envisioned spending the rest of my working years serving Gangaji with my family of friends. However, during the recession, to reduce costs, my position was eliminated, and my duties reassigned to my best friend.

Although I certainly didn't recognize it at the time, this loss was the perfect catalyst. All I could perceive was betrayal–by my friends, by my community, by my beloved teacher. Some days I could barely get out of bed. No previous insight–no practice, no experience–could relieve my grief and disillusionment. I thought I'd understood the guidance of Gangaji's teacher, Papaji, to "call off the search." But now I really called off the search. In this desert of despair, I built a bonfire fed by every teaching I'd acquired. Only what I could directly discern–directly experience as truth–survived the blaze.

Kicked out of the nest, in a free fall, I watched my familiar defensive impulses attempt to repel the raging waves of grief, of anger, of fear. Pushed to the edge, careening over the edge, in this intensity I discovered a new layer of the capacity to observe I'd first discovered with the Tibetans. Almost imperceptibly, a sober dispassion, born of an inner-directed compassion, loosened my resistance. Moment by moment, bit by bit, I softened to the raw intensity of my grief. It was simply the only thing left to do.

For months, over and over and over again, for brief moments, I opened as much as possible to each wave. Not indulging, not repressing. Not running from the storm. Not fighting or fleeing. Observing the intensity of the storm–this primal signal of distress, of disturbance.

Then one day, as I was wiping fingerprints from the refrigerator door, in the tiniest sliver of a moment, the intensity of my emotionality, even my repelling of the intensity, was simply another manifestation of potentiality–empty-fullness–simply another arising of my state of consciousness, of this me. Hiding in plain sight. Exactly as the Tibetans had described, overlooked, because it's too simple, too obvious, too close.

The Mahamudra text Khenpo Tsultrim taught compared a glimpse of clarity to the relief experienced when turning on the light in a darkened room and recognizing that the deadly snake coiled in the corner of the room, ready to strike, is only a piece of rope. I'd so desperately tried every technique, every practice I could find, attempting to banish the piece of rope masquerading as a snake—not recognizing it as simply another arising of consciousness (just as Kalu Rinpoche had described), not recognizing the portal-like invitation calling this imagined separate me back into itself.

With fresh eyes, I began revisiting the teachings I'd abandoned, finding previously unrecognized expressions of truth in the myriad descriptions of the inexpressible—in the Buddhist Mahamudra, in the Advaita teachings of Gangaji, Papaji, and Ramana Maharshi, in the Bible's stories of the life and teachings of Jesus. I explored the poetry of Rumi, Hafiz, and Kabir and the writings of the Christian mystics.

Words I'd first recited in a Baptist church and concepts I'd first learned there were unexpectedly illuminated when I accepted a friend's invitation to a weekday-night healing ceremony at a small Catholic church. The shiny slick wood of the pews were reminiscent of those in Oklahoma's Baptist church. The palpable silence carried the same resonance of that Baptist church, and of Kalu Rinpoche's room, of the monastery's shrine rooms, of my room in retreat. As I settled into the pew and closed my eyes, I was permeated by that stillness. This was a familiar, well-practiced cue to open to the ever-present compassion of the beloved, to the inconceivable divine. My visualization, my representation of this presence was now an amalgam of the loving presence of Kalu Rinpoche and Ramana Maharshi.

After resting in silence for ten or fifteen minutes, we were invited to file, row by row, to the front of the sanctuary to receive a blessing and healing. When my row stood, a woman sitting in the row directly behind me tapped my shoulder. When I turned, she whispered, "Thank you for bringing the Holy Spirit."

Returning to the Buddhist teachings, I resurrected my Shangri-La view of Tibetan divinely inspired purity. Although tarnished by the revelations of Kalu Rinpoche's secret sexual activities, this idealization survived for several more years. But that illusion was shattered when Kalu Rinpoche's now twenty-one-year-old reincarnation posted a video on YouTube.

Dressed in an army-green hooded parka, he haltingly described the sexual abuse he experienced when he was twelve and thirteen years old–by the very monks tasked with his education and care. Staring directly into the camera, his shoulders framed in a halo of fake fur, he revealed that his teacher had attempted to kill him.

I viewed his video repeatedly, now keenly aware how every human, even the apparently enlightened, can believe self-serving thoughts to be awakened thoughts. But then, hasn't the danger of slippery justification, of blindly causing harm, always existed in every tribe, every society, every religion? But if the messenger is flawed, is the message also flawed? Is it possible to find an unflawed messenger?

Even this shocking disclosure by Kalu Rinpoche's reincarnation could not, did not, prepare me for the next revelation. While searching the internet, checking in on Lama Norlha and the monastery, a link to an article authored by Lama Willa Baker popped into my browser. I knew this was Palmo. No longer using the name given to her by Kalu Rinpoche when we received our vows in Bodh Gaya, she was Willa again–Lama Willa. As I raced through the words of her narrative, a heavy dread rose up in my throat and weighed against my chest.

She'd written about our trip to India to receive vows. On our way to Kalu Rinpoche's monastery, we stopped for the night at a hotel in Delhi. She described how Lama had invited her to his room for a "dharma talk." After exchanging a few niceties, he grabbed her body and pressed his face into hers. This was the beginning of years of sexual exploitation, a relationship requiring birth control.

I recalled my encounter with Lama Norlha in the hallway of this same hotel in Delhi. He'd stood uncomfortably close while offering to take care of me "in any way I might need." I remembered sitting hip-to-hip with him in the rickshaw while traveling to the market to purchase butter for Kalu Rinpoche.

Reading, then re-reading Willa's words, my heart compressed with a darkly silent "no."

Her story described how she had wanted to speak openly about this sexual relationship with Lama Norlha, but he warned that doing so would break her samaya and bring shame on her, on him, and on the monastery. Her devotion compelled her to comply with his wishes. Finally, after fifteen years, after completing two three-year retreats, she left Lama and the monastery, earned a doctorate in religion from Harvard, and established her own Dharma Fellowship teaching program and retreat center. Still, she continued to maintain the secrecy Lama Norlha commanded. But when a young nun from the monastery called asking for her advice, their shared experiences tumbled out.

With newfound clarity, Willa initiated a public disclosure meeting at the monastery, facilitated by a professional mediator. Six women came forward and openly acknowledged Lama's no-longer-secret sexual life. In failing health, Lama Norlha didn't attend the meeting but sent a taped apology. He was removed from his position as head of the monastery and died ten months later.

Scanning my memories, I recalled overhearing Lama ask Willa to stop by his room to pick up his laundry. I'd been jealous that he never asked me to help with his laundry, not recognizing this was his code for "come to my room for sex." I'd not been able to see how protected I had been, how lucky I was not a favorite. I'd certainly recognized Lama's ruthlessness and experienced his justification of any action he deemed to be beneficial, but I never suspected he could take advantage of any student's innocent devotion.

Finally, finally, I was able to see Willa as someone to emulate, as my teacher, as an inspiration. Her words and her actions so clearly demonstrate the possibility of compassionately holding both the harmer and the harmed, while clearly denouncing the harmfulness.

This removal of another illusion, another disillusionment, was one more invitation to a party I can only attend while standing in my own shoes and trusting a still, small knowing–another dive into the muck to claim the gem, another opportunity to spin moldy straw into gold. With an ever-deepening respect for the ruthless grace of this life, of this journey, I recalled Gangaji's recounting of her teacher's, Papaji's, words of caution, "Vigilance until the last breath." Vigilance, not as a strategy of avoidance. Not as a wish for only sunny days. But the vigilance of remaining aware as waves of the challenges of living in this human form continue to rise and fall.

Opening into this awareness continues to be an ongoing practice. When turmoil hits and awareness wanes, I can be overtaken by emotional amnesia. I can forget the still home of my heart, lose track of the ground of unlimited awareness which always remains fundamentally unperturbed. I again identify as the "me" in this dream, attempting to grasp with ashen knuckles some imagined safety bar of the ride.

Yet, as I rest in the quiet of my bubbling water fountain, held in the deepest nourishment where the true beloved resides, in the wordless wedding of the known with what can never be known, thoughts and memories quietly ripple. For a moment it seemed they were calling me to a deeper well, a well not yet experienced–but it is not so. The deep well is simply here, always right here. Those thoughts, those seekings for understanding, are just vestiges of my mind, the record player running itself down. The ongoing story of this life–this perfect teacher, this arising of my state of consciousness, this grand mystery–continues to unfold. After all, I remain on this ride through time and space in my person-house body.

From the stillness of my brocaded chair, once again I become aware of the possibility of turning to face the apparent solidity–no, it can't be faced. There is a turning–no, actually nothing is done. There is only the truth of the shattering stillness of this moment. And in this truth, in this raging quiet, there is the arising, the continual endless arising of this story, of every story leading again and again to the truth of never lost, already found, already home.

ACKNOWLEDGEMENTS

When I first began writing this memoir more than a decade ago, I imagined working alone. I thought it might take a year—after all, I'd written a self-help book in under four months with just one round of edits. But I soon discovered that a memoir is a very different kind of book, one that demands not only writing skills I didn't yet possess, but also the courage to write with a vulnerability I didn't know how to access. More than once, I gave up. The truth is, this memoir exists only because of the support, guidance, critique, and encouragement of teachers, mentors, colleagues, and friends.

When I read author acknowledgments thanking long lists of people and insisting they couldn't have finished without them, I assumed it was polite exaggeration. Now I understand. Although writing this memoir began as a solitary act, finishing it required a community—friends who read drafts, listened as I read aloud, urged greater honesty, and reminded me that slow progress isn't failure but an essential part of the creative process—with its inevitable fallow periods.

When I first realized I needed help, I found writing teacher Laura Davis. She and the participants in her classes and workshops repeatedly challenged me to write with more vulnerability and honesty. Susan Brown, a guest teacher in a few of those workshops, offered clear instruction on how to construct scenes, shift through time, and craft strong openings and closings. Not only were her teachings invaluable, but the title of this memoir, *Girl in a Box*, came from her.

Next, writing coach Annie Tucker guided me through creating a rough draft. With her encouragement, I was able to weave scattered fragments, vignettes, and musings into something whole. Then the editing process could begin.

I was fortunate to find editor Cher Johnson, who brought both a skilled editorial eye and deep respect for what I was trying to convey. She polished–and in doing so inspired me to polish. She stripped away excess, pressed for clarity, and reminded me to "show, not tell."

After Cher and I combed through the manuscript chapter by chapter, Carla Sherman's sharp eye caught typos, stray commas, and formatting quirks.

I'm grateful to friends including Cat Rowland, Mareijke Weidemann, and Carla Sherman, who listened as I read sections aloud during the editing. Pam Carraher spent many hours listening over the phone, helping me hear when the words didn't flow.

Once I had a draft ready for beta readers, Tim Andersson, Coralie Murray, Diane Peterson, Judy McCall, Tiffin Howard, Dale Webb, Joanna Quintrell, Shelley Galvan, Murray Kennedy, Alumine Kennedy, Trinley Tambor, Daniel Brown, and Bruce Swanson offered feedback and encouragement, giving me the confidence to share the book more widely. I'm also grateful for the beta reader insights from talented writers Kathy Crizik, Veronica Robinson, Emily Conway, and Linda Albert. Luvia Swanson generously read and commented not only on the original draft but also on the final version. I'm especially grateful to Gayle Brenner for her generous feedback and support.

I'm grateful for the support of Kathe Mitchell, Ryan McNabb, Germaine Bennison, John Bennison, Colleen Gonzales, Susan

Puetz, Christine Holmstrom, Chris Johns, and each person in my Spiritual Direction community.

And I'm deeply grateful to my husband, George, for his support during every stage of this long process.

I'm also grateful to Jon Sweeney and Monkfish Publishing for recognizing the potential of this book, for their guidance in shaping it for publication, and for creating such a beautiful cover design.

This book would not exist if I'd never encountered the wisdom of the Tibetan teachings. Words cannot capture my awe for the grace of that exposure. Then, meeting Gangaji and spending so many years in the shelter of her transmission of Ramana's presence further supported the unfolding of that grace. While writing this memoir, books by Karla McLaren, Richard Rohr, Cynthia Bourgeault, James Finley, Elaine Pagels, Pema Chödrön, Yongey Mingyur Rinpoche, Andrew Holecek, Beatrice Chestnut, Paul Levy, Carlo Rovelli, and Adyashanti provided confirmation and inspiration, helping to unravel and describe my deepening recognition of the gifts of those years spent with the Tibetans.

LIST OF CHARACTERS

Tibetans

Chögyam Trungpa Rinpoche (1939-87)
Born in Eastern Tibet, he was recognized as a prominent spiritual leader at a young age. After receiving a scholarship to study at Oxford in England, he observed stark differences between Eastern and Western cultures. Without the support of his lineage, he began adapting traditional Tibetan teachings to bridge this cultural gap in a way that would resonate with Western audiences. Even though I never actually met Chögyam Trungpa Rinpoche, he appears in my memoir multiple times.

Lama Norlha (1938-2018)
Lama Norlha was the abbot of Kagyu Thubten Chöling Monastery and Retreat Center. Born in Tibet, he grew up in a monastery. In 1976, at the request his teacher, Kalu Rinpoche, he moved to New York City where he taught Buddhist philosophy and meditation practices. Two years later, he founded the monastery and retreat center on seven acres of land overlooking the Hudson River in Wappingers Falls, New York.

Kalu Rinpoche (1905-89)
Kalu Rinpoche was Lama Norlha's teacher and the spiritual head of Kagyu Thubten Chöling Monastery and Retreat Center. When not traveling, he resided at his home monastery in Sonada, India. Recognized as one of the great meditation masters of the Buddhist tradition, he was known for his emphasis on meditation practice.

Jamgon Kongtrul Rinpoche (1954-92)
Jamgon Kongtrul Rinpoche was one of the four regents (heart-sons) of the Karmapa, the head of the Kagyu lineage of Tibetan Buddhism. He appears briefly in the memoir when he visits the monastery.

Dilgo Khyentse Rinpoche (1910-91)
Recognized as one of the greatest realized Buddhist masters of our time, he was the head of the Nyingma lineage of Tibetan Buddhism from 1988 until his death. Dilgo Khyentse Rinpoche also appears briefly in the memoir at the cremation ceremony for Chögyam Trungpa Rinpoche.

Khenpo Tsultrim Gyamtso Rinpoche (1934-2024)
Khenpo Tsultrim Gyamtso Rinpoche was an eminent master and scholar of the Kagyu lineage of Tibetan Buddhism teaching widely in the West. He visited the monastery to present teachings on Mahamudra.

Westerners

Dan
Dan is my first teacher in Oklahoma. He's a renaissance man–a playwright, piano player, singer, guitar adept, sculptor, painter ... and my spiritual guide.

Roberta (Trinley)

Roberta is my best friend from Oklahoma. When she takes vows as a Tibetan Buddhist nun, she receives the name Trinley. She's the steady, contemplative seeker of wisdom I so wished I could be.

Dechi

Dechi is one of the nuns who lives at the monastery. She taught me how to tape and spackle sheetrock when I was first visiting.

Willa (Palmo)

Willa first visited the monastery while she was a student at nearby Vassar College. She received the name Palmo when she took vows as a Tibetan Buddhist nun. She's the exemplar of the ideal student and nun who Lama Norlha encourages me to emulate.

Drupten

Drupten is one of the monks living at the monastery. He completed a three-year retreat and serves as a Tibetan language instructor.

Jodi (Chodrin)

Jodi returned to the monastery to prepare for a three-year retreat after earning a nursing degree. She became Chodrin when she took vows as a Tibetan Buddhist nun.

Pema Chödrön

A renowned Tibetan Buddhist nun, teacher, and author known for her teachings on mindfulness, compassion, and living fearlessly. Born in 1936 in New York City, she embraced Buddhism in her forties and studied under Chögyam Trungpa Rinpoche. As the former director of Gampo Abbey, she guided a monastic community and taught Buddhism to diverse audiences. Her influential books and practical approach have made her one of the most respected Buddhist teachers of our time.

Tsupa

Tsupa was one of Lama Norlha's first students and one of his favorites. She helped construct the monastery's buildings including the two retreat houses. She's the designated student leader and Lama Norlha's translator in the women's retreat in which Trinley is participating.

GLOSSARY OF TIBETAN TERMS

Bardo: The intermediate state between death and rebirth according to Tibetan Buddhist beliefs. It is a transitional phase where the consciousness transitions from one life to another.

Bodhisattva: A being who has attained enlightenment but remains in the cycle of birth and death to help others achieve liberation.

Bön: The indigenous religion of Tibet, which predates the introduction of Buddhism.

Chenrezig: A deity considered to be the embodiment of the compassion of all Buddhas.

Chöpon: A ritual master or attendant in Tibetan Buddhist ceremonies. They assist in performing rituals, maintaining the sacred space, and supporting the spiritual teacher.

Cho Tor: A practice of making offerings.

Chod: A spiritual practice in Tibetan Buddhism that involves cutting through the ego and offering one's body as a feast to deities and spirits.

Dahl: A type of lentil soup or stew commonly eaten in South Asia.

Daka: Often translated as "sky dancer" or "sky walker," dakas are associated with the skillful means of transformation and are considered to be the embodiment of wisdom and compassionate energy. They are known for their ability to transcend conventional boundaries and social norms in order to assist others in their spiritual journey. Dakas are often depicted as fierce, wrathful figures, symbolizing their power to overcome obstacles and ignorance on the path to awakening.

Dakini: A female deity or enlightened being in Tibetan Buddhism associated with transformation and spiritual awakening.

Dak nang: Pure view.

Dharma: The teachings and doctrines of Buddhism. It encompasses the principles and practices that lead to spiritual awakening and liberation.

Dharmapalas: The protective deities or guardians of the Buddhist teachings. They are enlightened beings who protect and preserve the Dharma, as well as guide practitioners on their spiritual paths.

Dorje Sempa: Also known as Vajrasattva, a bodhisattva deity associated with purification and the removal of negative karma.

Dukkha: A Pali term commonly translated as "suffering" or "unsatisfactoriness," one of the central concepts in Buddhism.

Gao: A hollow pendant filled with tiny packets of blessed substances ready to be ingested as a quick blessing in the event of impending death.

Gelong: A Tibetan Buddhist monk who has taken full ordination.

Gelongma: The female equivalent of a gelong, a fully ordained Tibetan Buddhist nun.

Gelug: One of the four major schools of Tibetan Buddhism, known as the Gelugpa or "Yellow Hat" sect. The Dalai Lama is the head of the Gelugpa sect of Tibetan Buddhism.

Gyalings: A type of traditional Tibetan wind instrument used in Buddhist rituals and ceremonies.

Hinayana: A term used by some schools of Buddhism to refer to the early or "lesser" vehicle.

Kagyu: One of the major schools of Tibetan Buddhism, known for its emphasis on meditation and direct realization.

Kangling: A traditional Tibetan instrument made from a human thigh bone, used in Chod practices.

Karma: The law of cause and effect, the ethical principle that governs actions and their consequences in Buddhism.

Karmapa: The title given to the head of the Karma Kagyu school of Tibetan Buddhism.

Kata: A ceremonial silk scarf used as a gesture of respect and blessing.

Khenpo: An advanced scholar and teacher in Tibetan Buddhism, often responsible for teaching and overseeing monastic education.

Kyorpon: An advanced scholar, a Doctor of Divinity.

Lama: A Tibetan title used for a spiritual teacher or guru in Buddhism.

Lhakhang: Shrine room, the sanctuary.

Mahamudra: A meditation practice in Tibetan Buddhism that focuses on direct realization of the nature of mind. It is a path to achieving enlightenment through recognizing the fundamental nature of one's own mind.

Mahasiddha: A practitioner in Tibetan Buddhism who has attained high levels of spiritual realization and extraordinary powers.

Mahasukha: Great bliss.

Mahayana: One of the three major branches of Buddhism, emphasizing compassion and the path of the bodhisattva.

Mala: A string of beads used for counting repetitions of prayers or mantras.

Mandala: A sacred and symbolic geometric design representing the universe or a particular deity. They are used as a means to connect with the energies and qualities represented by the deity, as well as to generate spiritual insights and awakenings.

Mantra: A sacred sound, word, or phrase repeated during meditation or as part of a spiritual practice.

Momos: A type of Tibetan dumplings usually filled with meat or vegetables.

Nirvana: The ultimate goal of Buddhist practice. It refers to the state of liberation, freedom from suffering, and the cessation of the cycle of birth, death, and rebirth.

Nyingma: The oldest of the four major schools of Tibetan Buddhism, known for its emphasis on the ancient or "original" teachings.

Ngöndro: Preliminary practices in Tibetan Buddhism, includes prostrations, recitations, and visualizations.

Oo-kor: A circular breathing technique used in playing wind instruments involving inhaling through the nose while exhaling through the mouth to maintain a continuous airflow.

Pecha: A Buddhist religious text or scripture.

Phowa: The practice of training for the transfer of consciousness to a pure Buddha-field at the time of death.

Puja: This refers to a devotional practice or ceremony in Tibetan Buddhism. It involves offering prayers, chants, mantras, and various rituals to deities or enlightened beings as a way to accumulate merit and cultivate spiritual qualities.

Rag-dung: Deep, droning bass horns which telescope out to eight feet. The rag-dung horn is played by blowing air into it while manipulating the sound with the lips and fingers. It produces a deep, resonant sound that is believed to have a purifying and transformative effect. The sound of the rag-dung horn is used to invoke the presence of deities, clear negative energies, and create a sacred atmosphere during rituals, pujas, and other spiritual activities.

Rolmo: A ritual cymbal with a broad central dome.

Sakya: One of the major schools of Tibetan Buddhism. It was founded in the eleventh century and is known for its emphasis on scholasticism and the study of Buddhist philosophy.

Samaya: The sacred vows and commitments made by practitioners in Vajrayana Buddhism. These vows are considered essential for maintaining a close relationship with one's teacher and the lineage.

Samsara: Refers to the cyclic existence of birth, death, and rebirth in Buddhism. It represents the realm of suffering and dissatisfaction that sentient beings continuously experience until they attain liberation.

Sankhara-Dukkha: A term used in Buddhism to describe the unsatisfactoriness or suffering that arises from conditioned existence. It refers to the inherent dissatisfaction and impermanence found in all conditioned phenomena.

Silnyen: A ritual cymbal with a small or no central dome.

Shamthap: The skirt part of Tibetan monastic robes, a tube of seven yards of fabric.

Stupa: A Buddhist monument or shrine that represents the enlightened mind of the Buddha. It typically consists of a mound or dome-shaped structure containing relics or sacred objects, and it serves as a focal point for meditation and veneration.

Tantrayana: Also known as Vajrayana. A branch of Buddhism that emphasizes esoteric practices and techniques to attain enlightenment. It employs rituals, visualizations, and mantra recitation as means to transform ordinary experiences into spiritual awakening.

Tara: A female deity in Tibetan Buddhism. She is considered a bodhisattva, the mother of the Buddhas, and is associated with compassion, protection, and swift action. She is often depicted in various forms and colors, each representing different qualities and aspects.

Thangka: A Tibetan Buddhist painting on cotton or silk fabric. It typically depicts deities, buddhas, or scenes from religious narratives. Thangkas serve as objects of devotion, meditation aids, and tools for transmitting Buddhist teachings.

Tingshas: Small Tibetan cymbals, joined by a cord, that produce a clear, high-pitched tone when struck together.

Tonga: The vest part of Tibetan monastic robes constructed using two shades of burgundy fabric, with wing-like flaps at the shoulders. The tongas worn by senior lamas often have golden yellow cloth or sometimes ornate silk brocade for the front panels.

Tormas: Sculpted offerings made from various substances such as butter, barley flour, or dough. They are commonly used in Tibetan

Buddhist rituals and ceremonies as offerings to deities, spirits, or enlightened beings.

Tulku: A recognized reincarnate lama or spiritual teacher. It is believed that certain highly realized individuals can consciously choose to be reborn to continue their spiritual work for the benefit of others.

Tummo: A practice of generating heat to raise one's internal body temperature.

Vajradhara: A deity in Vajrayana Buddhism, often considered the primordial Buddha or the ultimate embodiment of enlightenment. Vajradhara represents the unification of wisdom and compassion.

Vajrayana: Also known as Tantrayana. A branch of Buddhism that originated in India and is prominent in Tibetan Buddhism. It emphasizes the use of skillful means, rituals, and esoteric practices to achieve enlightenment in a single lifetime.

Vajrayogini: A prominent female deity in Tibetan Buddhism. She represents the union of wisdom and compassion. Her practice involves visualization, mantra recitation, and meditation. Engaging in her practice is believed to lead to spiritual transformation, realization of one's true nature, and the attainment of Buddhahood in a single lifetime. She is associated with overcoming attachment and the dualistic nature of ordinary existence.

Yab-yum: A Tibetan term that literally means "father-mother." It refers to a sacred tantric practice in which a male deity (father) and a female deity (mother) are depicted in an intimate embrace.

It symbolizes the union of wisdom and compassion, as well as the indivisible nature of masculine and feminine principles.

Yak: A large, long-haired bovine found in the Himalayan region. They are valued for their milk, meat, hair, and strength and are often associated with high-altitude living and endurance.

Zabuton: a traditional cushion that is used for sitting or kneeling. It is typically a flat, rectangular cushion filled with cotton, kapok, or foam and covered with fabric.

Zen: The burgundy shawl-like wrap of Tibetan monastic robes.

PALDROM CATHARINE COLLINS' introduction to religion was at the First Baptist Church she attended with her parents, until she left as a young woman seeking enlightenment–first in the mystical practices of the Tibetan Buddhist Vajrayana, then for fourteen years immersed in the non-dual teachings of Gangaji, in the Hindu Advaita lineage of Ramana Maharshi. Today, she's found a connection to contemplative Christianity, serving on the board of directors of the Journey Center Association, and completing their two-year spiritual director certification program.

Paldrom and her husband, George, live in California's San Francisco Bay Area. Their business, Neulia-Compulsion Solutions, provides counseling services for sex and porn addicts and their partners. In 2011, their book *A Couple's Guide to Sexual Addiction: A Step-by-Step Plan to Rebuild Trust & Restore Intimacy* was published by Adams Media. She's also authored articles published in *Inquiring Mind* and *Buddhadharma* (*Lion's Roar*) magazines.

We are

Monkfish Book Publishing

...an independent press publishing spiritual and literary books from a diverse range of perspectives. Genres include memoirs, wisdom literature, fiction, and scholarly works of thought. Monkfish books appeal to the seasoned or novice seeker as well as to the general public looking for reliable sources on spirituality. The readers we had in mind when we began Monkfish in 2002 were devoted spiritual seekers, the type whose passion for the spiritual quest would lead them to read across a dazzling array of traditions: Buddhist, Hindu, Jewish, Christian, Muslim, Native American and more. It has always been our intent to publish works of spiritual authenticity for the general public as well as the specialist and scholar.

Our books are available from booksellers everywhere.

Use this QR code to see recently published books:

Use this one to sign-up for our monthly newsletter:

www.ingramcontent.com/pod-product-compliance
Lightning Source LLC
Jackson TN
JSHW021524100326
99065JS00001B/329